Bearing THE BIG H

A
Hormonal
Journey
On The
Hysterectomy
Highway

by
Patti Pfeiffer

ISBN 0-9713881-0-5

First printing............March 2002

Printed in the U.S.A. by
Morris Publishing
3212 East Highway 30
Kearney, NE 68847

This book would only be a pile of papers, a ponderous paper wad if not for the pushing, prodding and persuading of my friend, lover and my one-man-cheering-squad my dear, loving husband Kenny—my compass, my anchor and my sail.

"A desire accomplished is sweet to the soul."
(Prov. 13:19 KJV)

Contents

Acknowledgements

To say it takes a lot to bring this literary undertaking to fruition is a true understatement.

First and foremost, I thank my doctor, surgeon and friend, RH for his handiwork, his skillful scalpel, and providing me the very topic for this book.

I want to thank the readers, subjected throughout the years to my writings, for all their literary reviews and critiques—the comments, the compliments and the criticisms.

Thanks to my mother, Guyla Pfeiffer and brother Matt, for giving me the stuff memories are made of—and books are written about.

My deepest appreciation goes to my "G.E.M." of a friend Sandra Dickey for her motivational jealousy, her professional and personal advice, and her many words of encouragement.

Also I wish to thank my many friends who stood with me, and by me—cheering, encouraging, and compelling me to complete this long endeavor. I am blessed to have such loving friends, too many to list. A special thanks to my warm-hearted, loving P.C. friends, especially "Uncle FJ" for the raisin'.

My friend brave enough, patient enough, bored enough, and crazy enough to offer and then actually complete her proofing assignments I thank from the bottom of my heart—Tammy Yates.

Thanks also to Debbe Taylor and KOR for all the years, all the help.

My deepest gratitude to Michelle Pfeiffer the sister I never had and a true shining star. Thank you for caring, for taking the time, and for aiming for true perfection.

Finally I thank my Editor-in-Chief for the daily guidance and blessing me with the courage, creativity and confidence necessary to make this dream become reality.

Preface

The title of this book was not the result of my creativity, nor was it an accident. It was the result of a caring gesture at a delicate moment. Before surgery, my husband gave me a cute, cuddly teddy bear with heart-shaped paw pads to comfort me during recovery. While recuperating in my hospital room, my doctor came in and noticed my brown, furry friend snuggled tightly in my arms. He asked to borrow the bear. Reluctantly, I handed over my soft sidekick. Then they both disappeared, only to return moments later. When I welcomed my buddy back, I noticed something different about her. My bear now bore a white bandage on her tummy resembling the one on my stomach. We were twins. However, my counterpart was spared the surgical sufferings and did not "Bear the Big H."

While a nonfiction book, my husband claims several stories within these pages are exaggerated. I flatly deny such an allegation! Maybe, I embellished, embossed, and enlarged a smidgen here and there for effect, but it was rare. My spouse would claim such a thing; he is after all the target (I mean topic) of many of the unflattering tales within. He has even goes as far as affectionately calling some contents "husband-bashing" material!

It is not my intent to poke fun at any profession, bully any business, insult individuals, grind any group or criticize any cause—hurt or harm anyone, anything, anywhere. I believe strongly in laughter and its ability to turn a sulk into a shining smile; its contagious nature and its healing benefits. For this reason, I've attempted to transform a serious subject (as well as the associated trials and tribulations) into entertaining, and light reading material.

I am no doctor, not even a nurse. The medical things I have learned, I learned firsthand. My medical knowledge, not to mention my overall knowledge, is quite limited, some might say. I know just enough to be dangerous in several areas. I make no qualms about it.

This is not a medical book. It is not intended to dispense medical advice or "make" a statement. Neither is it meant to take a positive or negative stand on hysterectomies. Likewise, it is not intended to sway possible patients one way or the other. Having a hysterectomy is a very personal decision, one that takes careful consideration and proper medical advice.

The purpose of this literary undertaking is very simple. I wanted to share with other women the highs, the lows, the peaks, and the pits of not only having a hysterectomy, but of being a woman. It is my hope that this book causes readers to laugh at me, at themselves, at life in general. Also, I want women to know that they are never alone in what they feel, what they think, and what they are. It is amazing how comforting those two little words "me too" can be.

It is sharing that prompted me to tell my tales on very personal subjects, in a very public format. While reading these pages, if one woman finds comfort, cracks a smile, or comments "me too," this book will have fulfilled its purpose; the author attained her goal.

I am Woman,
Hear Me Groan

Fasten your seatbelts! You are in for a wild ride through womanhood. Along the way there will be highs and lows, potholes and pitfalls, peaks and valleys—some foreign, others frighteningly familiar. Through the fertile forest of feminine foes, over puberty peaks, across the minefields of menstruation mania, and around rocky relational ravines this trip will encompass it all.

As major as it may be to me, my personal medical mayhem does not involve much complexity. Rather, it all boils down to three little medical terms: endometriosis, laparoscopy, and laser surgery. Based upon my own experience, I now think of these as terms of endurance. After two decades, I have grown accustomed to them. Those three things, singularly or combined, can all be classified simply as pains in my side, not to mention other unspeakable parts of my anatomy.

It all began so very long ago, before I was an apple in anyone's eyes. Beginning thousands of years before my momma and daddy were even apple seedlings themselves. Speaking of apples, I believe the core of my pain involves an apple and a story that goes something like this: In the beginning there was man, then woman, and true to her gender she was tempted by food, more accurately by an apple . . . (I'm certain if she ate fruit, chocolate hadn't yet been created!).

One little bite later and voila, there you have it—the creation of the whole female phenomenon, menstruation, premenstrual syndrome, cramps, intense pain, and all the other womanly wonders. Eve's legacy is a special one in that it has not only survived the test of time, but reaches so far and wide that it continues to touch all of us fortunate enough to be of that special gender. The walk on the moon was nothing compared to Eve and her actions. Truly one small bite for womankind!

However, if we were all going to have to suffer for her sin, I wish I could have at least had a say in the fruit. Apples give me gas. A banana (split) would have been more tempting! At any rate, that was the beginning of the trials and tribulations of womanhood, plain and simple. Luckily, my specific dilemma does not date quite that far back.

I am not too old (yet) that I cannot recall my younger days. That was the time when, as a mere naive girl, I actually waited and anticipated the onset of the entire puberty process. It's still fresh in my mind, like it was yesterday. Oh, I was so excited as I listened intensely to my friends relay their first menstruation experience, that rite of passage, the crossing of the bridge from girlhood to womanhood.

I admit my jealousy of those girl friends that made the journey before me. Every bragging conversation of "guess what happened to me yesterday?" was a crashing blow to my fragile, scrawny, teenage ego, and believe me, there was not much to blow away.

Again and again I listened as my friends bragged of the intimate details of their blossoming. If they were really my friends they would have spared me. Every day the circle of those who considered themselves "women" enlarged, while the rest of us late bloomers seemed to just wither on the vine.

In the silence and the safety of my bedroom, I would wonder about my own femininity. That would eventually give way to worries of when I, too, would be blessed with the passage.

The questions buzzed around my head like a swarm of bees. When would I start my period? Why wasn't it me this time? What is wrong with me? Why is everyone else so far ahead of me? But with each question came the sting of a silent answer.

Oh, the agony of being just a girl when all those around you are budding and blooming. I was at a loss as to what to do. There I was benched, sent to the sexuality sidelines, a mere spectator while everyone but me was growing up and out becoming mature girls, with mature bodies that made them major focal points (targets) for mature boys on the puberty-prowl.

Mother Nature's failure to knock on my door sent me

into the silence and safety of my own little world. I retreated and withdrew from my peers for I was no longer part of their elite, enlightened group. It was months (which seemed like years) before that stubborn, evasive female entity, *Ms.* Nature, finally made her house call and blessed me with that thing called puberty. With that came the long awaited, much anticipated "period" and the chance to finally wear a Kotex pad and be fitted for a bra. These things, I was convinced, would change my life forever. And change it did. Only then I thought it would be a change for the better!

Over a *period* of time (a very short time, I might add) I eventually outgrew my misguided excitement about menstruation. I realized "menstruation mania" was some terrible illness I had contracted in high school and which ran rampant among teenyboppers. A brief encounter with feminine products could burst any teenager's bubble. Tampon or pad, flush or toss, scented, winged, curved, gathered or straight, thin or thick, moderate flow or heavy, to line or let linger. The possibilities were endless and sometimes overwhelming. I never really knew what to do, what to buy. Don't tell the manufacturers, but for me it always just came down to the most colorful and appealing packaging.

With time and age that lovely, life-altering event brought a huge dose of reality. Unfortunately, for me that meant pure and simple unadulterated pain. At the ripe old age of twenty-two I became woman-wise and learned two very important things. First was an educational introduction to endometriosis. Secondly, and far more important, was the fact that a male gynecologist is, above all else, only a man. Therefore, he is by his very nature incapable of completely understanding the finer (and unfortunately, most painful) points of being a woman. I discovered this fact quite by mistake during my first encounter with the endometriosis villain—a source of pain that was to saddle me for almost two decades.

To be honest, it was my first encounter with an uncaring and insensitive gynecologist that caused me to needlessly endure pain-filled periods for years. I remember that too, like it was yesterday.

My menstrual cycles were not periods but *occasions.*

They were times when my life, as I knew it, would come to an abrupt and screaming halt, giving way to pain and misery. Once a month I would fall victim to excruciating and debilitating anguish in my lower back and upper thighs. On these occasions I would seek relief in the form of prescription pain pills. I had run the gamut of all over-the-counter drugs to no avail. The pain always prevailed.

For the first year or two I just dealt with it, thinking this magnitude of pain was normal—just the price us women were forced to pay for some mistake that was made way back in some garden in the beginning of time. Eventually, I had enough of my pain and agony, bitching, moaning, and groaning. In desperation I finally made an appointment with a gynecologist in hopes of finding an answer, a solution to my painful periods. I honestly had no clue what, if anything, was causing me to "go down" a few days a month, but I needed to know if this degree of debilitation was indeed part of the *joy* of womanhood.

I arrived at the doctor's office full of apprehension and the examination did nothing to calm my nerves. While I was psyched up for something lengthy and thorough, the entire examination was short and seemingly routine. The doctor seemed unconcerned, inattentive, and even callous. In the end, he seemed to dismiss the physical exam entirely and focus more on his line of third-degree questioning. To my surprise, the final diagnosis hinged on a single question.

"Do you have pain with sexual intercourse?" he asked. I answered very honestly in the negative.

Based upon that response, I was nonchalantly dismissed with parting words that, to this day, are still fresh in my mind and strike not only a nerve, but a raw, exposed nerve.

"I thought maybe you had endometriosis; but if you do not have pain with intercourse, then you do not have endometriosis and there is nothing wrong. Therefore I can do nothing for you," he said.

"Is this type of pain normal?"

After all, it was the only thing I really wanted to know, the real reason I had made this trek to his examination table, the sole purpose of placing my feet in those nasty stirrups in the first place.

"No, I would think not. If the pain gets unbearable, come back and we can do a laparoscopy, but I doubt we will find anything."

Like I wasn't already in excruciating pain! Talk about feeling like a hypochondriac. Thinking my painful periods were normal and my low tolerance for pain the only thing abnormal, I left his office that day with a new and improved grin-and-bear-it attitude.

However, only a year later the smiles turned upside down and the pain worsened to the point that life between ovulation and menstruation was nothing short of miserable. I graduated from just popping pain pills. My periods had become so debilitating that in desperation I would stay home from work three to four days out of the month in a drug-induced slumber. In bed and doped up was the only way I could battle the internal beast that waged war within my female organs.

Having my painful pleas fall on a doctor's deaf ears, I felt I was my only ally and fighting in private my only option. I pledged to be the best soldier I could be, and sought strength in my own private peptalks.

Suffer and suffer alone. A little pain won't kill you. Quit whining all the time, my internal voice mocked at me. Other women endure this all the time, some surely without pills and without staying at home. Since this is normal, we too can withstand Mother Nature's rapture.

My doctor had made me feel so foolish for complaining about my pain that I sulked and suffered in silence. My pain was no big deal, I thought to myself. I would not seek medical help for anything so frivolous as a little menstruation discomfort. I now believed it was all in my head. What made me think I was so special? If other women could cope, so could I.

For the longest time I refused to seek medical assistance, afraid another doctor would also think I was just faking it. I could take anything but the faking routine; a family trait I vowed never to let become part of my own personality. I feared it, for it was in the genes. My grandmother was the type of person that sought medical attention just to get attention. Any attention was better than no attention. I never remember a time she wasn't sick, wasn't going to the doctor, or wasn't recovering from one ailment or another. From organ removals to appliance implants to big toe and even little toe amputation, she had run the spectrum of physical foes—and seemed to enjoy them all. Those memories kept me from seeking medical help, for more than my pain, I feared being branded with the same label as my grandmother. Therefore, I held on and held out as long as physically possible.

Twelve months later, out of sheer desperation, I finally fell in defeat. I sat on my bed that infamous day, crying uncontrollably. The realization set in, and I admitted to myself that I could not go on in my current, crippled manner. Physically, mentally, and emotionally wounded, I sought medical advice one more time. This time help came in the form of another doctor—fortunately one more competent, and more compassionate.

After an examination and consultation, it was decided that a laparoscopy was in order and, according to my newfound physician friend, was probably way past due. As is normal for that type of operation, I was scheduled for outpatient surgery. I was not apprehensive. I knew any discovery that led to some type of relief would be of great benefit to my body and me.

To make a long story short, the surgery turned into more of an ordeal than anyone had expected. Upon peering into my inners, a massive amount of endometriosis was indeed discovered The invasive barnacles had overtaken my organs, attaching themselves to anything they could cling to: my ovaries, my uterus, even slithering into my fallopian tubes. It all had been taken hostage by this rogue trespasser. I was a walking host to a persistent and painful pest.

It took hours for my doctor to remove the massive amounts of internal growths. The simple procedure was anything but simple. It was, in fact, so long in duration that an overnight hospital stay was required.

Upon hearing the news of this discovery, my first thought was of my former doctor and his callous attitude. I was so happy! I had been exonerated. It was a surgical vindication. I was innocent of being a hypochondriac. So thrilled, I wanted to shout from the hospital rooftops for all to hear: "I was full of endometriosis. It took hours for the doctor, with a handy dandy laser, to zap all that clung to me. Hours, I say. Oh, how beautiful it is. My pain was well-founded! Nah, nah, nah, nah, nah! It was not mental, and I am not whack-o." I had known it, and now everyone else would know it, too. My family, my boss, my friends, and yes, even my ex-doctor.

As one can see, it takes very little to make me happy. My first laser surgery was a snap and after a day or two, I was not only as good as new, I was better than I had been in years. To be barnacle-free was truly a life-altering experience.

However I was not "new" for long. This condition, this stuff, reminds me of some of my past boyfriends: stubborn, resistant, difficult to deal with, hard to get rid of, and even harder to forget completely.

Although not a doctor, I have become somewhat of an expert on endometriosis. There is no cure, only treatments that help. One such thing is pregnancy, although endometriosis itself can lead to infertility. Go figure, the one thing they say can curtail endometriosis is the one thing it prevents. Sounds like a real smart monster in that it's smart enough to eliminate that which can curtail it.

I had been told that birth control pills also help control endometriosis. Well, been there and done that. After taking the pill and blowing up a few dress sizes, I opted to dispense with the pink dispenser and roll the dice on a recurrence.

There is a good reason I don't gamble much. I always lose. This time proved to be no exception. I rolled the dice, and sure to form, I lost. Only the stakes were higher than money. Ten years later I was back in the operating room for the same procedure, with the same gynecologist.

In terms of a laparoscopy with laser, this too was a lengthy procedure because my "buddy," not lacking in determination, had come back with a vengeance this time he had fortified the barnacle building erected within me.

After the operation, my doctor spoke to my mother. In the waiting room he gave her some doctorly advice soon to be motherly advice. I guess he felt it was better coming from her, kind of a mother-daughter thing.

Bearing the Big H

According to my mom, the doctor felt there was a "Patti pattern" emerging, in that I was in need of surgery at least every ten years. In the doctor's opinion, this pattern, in all likelihood, would continue. According to his calculations, and given my current age of 32, the need for another laser surgery would occur sometime past childbearing age. Therefore, he suggested at that point I should consider opting for the whole ball of wax, the whole nine yards, none other than the Big H.

My mother, being the dutiful mom she is, did indeed deliver the message. Busy and about to bolt, I heard it, I ignored it, and I left the hospital. Like Scarlet O'Hara, I would worry about that tomorrow. It was such a long time away, another lifetime. Besides, I felt great and was ready to rock-n-roll.

Well, I rocked along for another few years. During that time I got married. Yeah, I am a real late bloomer. My bachelorette days taught me that it's more acceptable to be married and divorced several times than to be single in your mid-to late-thirties. I know that everyone was wondering what was wrong with this old girl! However, I resisted the proposals, stood my ground, and withstood the hairy, scary experience of living the single life in a major metropolitan area. I am proud to admit that I did not succumb to social pressure, but gave in only to the heart.

After years of dodging the bullet—better known as the institution of marriage—a man entered my life. He was not just any man, but one strong enough, resilient enough, and crazy enough to attempt to saddle this wild mare. He managed to corral me, slip that lasso over my head and around my neck, and the rest is his-story.

The engagement was short (to say the least) for two reasons. First and foremost, I knew he was the man for me. After years of doing things incorrectly and dating a long line of "Mr. Wrongs" I learned my lesson. At my age and at my level of experience, these life lessons had now finally turned into wisdom. It was time for the payoff.

So when someone different, the type just the opposite of those before, stumbled into my path, I wasted no time in changing my ways and my attitude—before I really did become an old maid! I was no longer a fool and blatantly

8

admit I wasted no time in getting my hooks into "Mr. Right" and reeling him in.

So with his marriage proposal came the decision of setting a wedding date—the second reason for a short engagement. With the wedding when-and-where decisions came the onset of worry and fear, more commonly referred to as cold feet. As I contemplated the details of the occasion, a long list of questions streamed through my mind, wrecking havoc on the decision-making process. Why would anyone want a wedding? Why tempt fate and test my nerves during such a grand (and huge) occasion? Why create a stage for cold feet to stomp across my courage? Hurry, hurry, hurry—why wait for the opportunity to crawfish out of this one? The quicker I say I do, the less likely I am to say I don't, I won't.

My heart was saying yes, but my bachelorette head was definitely saying, What? Me getting hitched, no way! So in order to avoid the panic, and with it the real likelihood of becoming a runaway bride as well as an old maid, I opted for the panic-preventive type of wedding: a simple, short, swift, cut-to-the-chase ceremony.

We were married a mere two weeks later. While the engagement was fleeting, the wedding was fabulous. In a serene setting at sunset, in an atmosphere of love, and surrounded only by immediate family, the wedding was material made for a romance novel.

How does this relate to the subject at hand? That can be answered very simply with one word, "honeymoon." Following in the footsteps of our engagement, our honeymoon was short lived because a problem soon arose between us: pain with intercourse.

Let me tell you, girlfriends, there is nothing worse than being a newlywed and having to explain to my new husband that he not only married me but also my constant companion, the one I had affectionately nicknamed *my barnacle buddy*. Unfortunately, my buddy took it upon himself to make the introductions, and did so with perfect timing, in a grand style.

The ink wasn't even dry on the marriage certificate when I was coming up with wifely excuses my husband had never heard before. It is one thing to have a headache once in a while, but quite another to tell your new husband he's causing you pain (more than usual) at every attempt to consummate the marriage.

Hindsight being what it is, I should have had my husband share the marriage vows with my constant internal companion. I could hear it now: "I promise to take you, Barnacle Buddy, as my wife's constant source of pain; to have and to tolerate from this day forth, in sickness and in pain; during intercourse as well as before, during and after menstruation; in times of remission and retreats; and in recurrence and rebounds until laser or hysterectomy do us all three part."

Having chosen to become a wife, and being a perfectionist, I wanted to be a great wife. So hiding under the cover of darkness I would bite my lip and occasionally whimper while simultaneously singing his praises and stroking his ego regarding his manly abilities and performance. There was no doubt in my mind that our bedroom had become a stage because this was indeed an act! Obviously I had missed my calling in life. I must be a natural as an actress, for my other half never knew the difference. Being a man, he just assumed the moaning was because he was so good. Silly boy!

Well, that all worked for a while, but fun I was NOT having. I couldn't understand why now, at this point in my life, when I was doing things right, why my body wasn't cooperating. It had only been two years since my last surgery and, according to my calculations, another dose of laser wasn't due for another eight more years, or so I thought. As usual, I was wrong. The unwelcome guest, which had taken up residency in my womb, was obviously claiming squatter's rights and was determined not to leave without a real knock-down-drag-out fight.

The time had come again. I could feel it. I knew it. Surgery was calling. The intimate part of marriage was becoming a hassle and a real painful part of our relationship. I hurt and my husband was in pain. He was amorous and in hot pursuit. I was elusive and in cold retreat. He wanted sexuality while I demanded sensitivity. He pleaded; I prolonged. He wanted a piece; I wanted peace. He tried to turn me on; I tried to tune him out. Sadly enough, within the first few months of our marriage, it was only in the silence of his sulking that I found satisfaction. He, on the other hand, equipped only with a very narrow, male definition of satisfaction, never quite found any.

In an attempt to keep the peace and preserve the marriage, I made an appointment with a local doctor. For the first time in my life I had left my home state of Texas and moved north, into what many of us Texans considered enemy territory—Oklahoma. Unfortunately, I could not talk my gynecologist into moving with me. For a woman who has chronic gynecological problems, the thought of being without the one who knows her best inside and out, is scary at the least.

Commuting to Texas for an office visit was definitely out of the question. I had no choice but to find an interim *foreign* gynecologist, one that would do until I got back across the Red River, back into Texas, the home of my tried and true gynecologist. Out of options, I found another doctor, reluctantly made the appointment, and then made the visit.

He seemed nice enough at first glance. And to his credit there were pictures on the ceiling of his examining room, which is really important to many women, including me. The time seems to pass faster, and the position seems much more bearable, when staring at something other than the boring blankness of a white ceiling.

After the examination, I relayed the information and advice my "real" doctor had suggested about eliminating the entire problem all together by having a hysterectomy. This was to be the turning point in our pleasant doctor-patient relationship. His counter, in my battle-scarred opinion, was rather quite insensitive. "There is not a limit to the number of laparoscopies you can have."

Oh, spoken just like a man, I thought to myself, restraining my tongue and dimming my deadly-dagger glare. Then and there the memories of my past gynecological encounters came flooding back.

However desperate for relief, I gave in to his suggestion. Once again I was heading back to the operating table. Back under the knife went my barnacle buddy and me. The barnacle got zapped and I got relief, however temporary it might be.

In the end, both my doctor and I were surprised. He was surprised to find the amount of endometriosis that had reappeared. I was surprised when only two months later I was back in his office, tired, teary-eyed, complaining of more pain than ever before and ready to surrender in complete defeat. I was not only waving the white flag, I was a walking white flag.

I was at my wits end, completely out of excuses for my anguish. Due to mood swings, I was a source of perpetual motion, giving the Energizer Bunny a run for his money. My life, my hormones, my body, and my pain were out of control. I began to consider my only alternative to be long-term commitment in a psychiatric hospital. Where could I go from here? After doing battle with my unwanted sidekick for half of my life, it seemed as though I had lost the war.

Back to square one—yet again. Only eight short weeks after the latest eradication attempt, I sat in the gynecologist's office. The doctor just looked at my husband and me, a blank stare painted on his face.

Finally, as if to fend off the silence, he made what seemed to be his final offer.

"I can do another laparoscopy if you want me to try again," he meekly offered.

Had I acted upon what I really wanted to do at that moment, I would have been sent to prison for a long, long time. Follow-up appointments were routine, par for the course, but postoperative operation? That was the beginning of the end for me. After consulting with my husband and reviewing my options, I opted to take yet another wait-and-see attitude. After all, I had just come through one surgery, and the idea of another so soon afterwards did nothing for me. Living with the pain was nothing new. However, the duration and magnitude of my pain now seemed to be increasing with each passing month.

Not surprisingly, the passage of time did not bring relief. My monthly vacation went from a three-day deal to a three-week ordeal. Ovulation became more of a hurdle than the actual period itself. Everything was out of whack. The mood swings, the depression, the personality changes, and the pain sent me on a mission to find what was causing the monthly metamorphosis I was undergoing.

Quite honestly, my search and recovery mission was not complicated at all. Actually it was rather simple. I was searching for an answer to the same question: What in the hell was causing this ugly transformation from wife to witch? With each doctor the complaint was the same, only the degree of desperation increased. First I went to an internal medicine doctor, with not much success. Then I tried another gynecologist. With no suitable answers, I sought the counsel of a therapist. Out of sheer desperation, I even visited a shrink (in a vain attempt to rule out the remote possibility that I might be out of my mind). The monologue was the same from office to office and couch to couch.

"This is not me. I am not myself. I have become a real witch," I complained again and again. "I don't know how my husband can stand me, because I can't stand myself. I need help and I don't know if my problem is mental, physical, emotional, or hormonal. Actually, it just doesn't matter as long as someone can help me and put a stop to this!" My plea became "Give me an answer and give me relief."

From doctor's office to doctor's office in three different cities within a one-year period, I pleaded my case. I was desperate for an answer, desperate for a cure in the form of HELP!

It was finally a woman MD who explained that, although I might be years from actual menopause, my hormone level was decreasing in preparation for this life-altering exit from the monthly obligations of womanhood.

"I hate to tell you this, but what you are experiencing will, in all likelihood, get worse over the next few years," she said.

If my marriage was to stay intact, that certainly was not an option. At stake were also my sanity, my family, and the few friends I had managed to hang onto to this point.

We discussed my options—and there weren't many to choose from. There were birth control pills to level my hormonal swings and/or antidepressants to battle the lowest of my array of mood swings. However, that old saying been there, done that definitely applied to all of her suggestions.

She was caring and understanding, and that in itself was some relief. After she finished outlining the few options, I broached the subject of the Big H. "How do you know when and if you should consider a hysterectomy?" I asked her. After listening to me describe my long bout with endometriosis and my

13

past surgeries, she was sympathetic to my cause.

"Only you can make the decision to have a hysterectomy," she pronounced like a true doctor. "When and if the time is right, then you'll *WANT* to have the surgery. If you tire of it all before Mother Nature makes her grand finale, you will know it."

At that moment I knew it. I didn't need any time to think this one through. It was a real no-brainer! After 18 years of hosting this unwanted and constant companion inside my uterus (even though surgically evicted three times) I decided that this villain medically known as endometriosis had to go. The time had come. It was me or it. I was ready, and *it* was going to be removed! I wasn't about to be outdone, conquered by some pesky and persistent parasite.

TWO

Barren Bound

When it comes to menstruation, I don't like Mother Nature. In my opinion she is fickle, unreliable, and oh-so stubborn. When I anticipated her arrival, she was late. When I demanded her departure, she stayed, even set up camp, becoming a permanent fixture in my life. I credit her with the "split" in my personality.

Making a decision is difficult for me. This, like so many other negative quirks in my biological makeup, I conveniently blame on genetics. Yeah, I know, me and the rest of the world. However, this really is a hereditary trait. My mother tears a piece of chewing gum in two and then can't decide on which half to chew!

However, given my past gynecological saga, the decision to part with the major portion of my female anatomy was an easy one to make. Having decided on a course of action, I now needed an accomplice, someone to do the dirty deed, someone to anatomically alter me. The role called for a Clint Eastwood-type to "Make my day," ridding me of the antagonist that stole the spotlight in this female flick in which I had unwillingly been cast.

I was not happy with the attitude of my current, local gynecologist; and the one I wanted was geographically undesirable. I considered all my options, including doctornapping. I had heard of the Mann Act, a Congressional act prohibiting transporting a woman across state lines for illicit purposes. However, I didn't think it would apply to carrying a doctor across a state border for surgical purposes.

Although feasible, traveling out of state to undergo surgery was not really plausible. It would be more of a hassle than the operation itself. Imagine how time-consuming postoperative appointments would be with a doctor five hundred miles away.

It was obvious therefore, that I should attempt to find another doctor nearby. Familiar with only one other local gynecologist, I turned to the man that had done magic on my mom. Unfortunately, her gynecologist happened to office with my current-and-soon-to-be-ex gynecologist.

To some, I am sure it appeared as if I was making the rounds at the doctors' office. This change was not an easy decision, for I feared being labeled a table-hopper. I could imagine the office staff speaking of my shopping for a physician: Will she ever settle down with one doctor? Is she going to see every gynecologist here before she decides on one? I have heard of doctors making the rounds, but never of a patient making the rounds.

Regardless of the fallout, I made another appointment within the same office, with yet another gynecologist. I honestly don't think the poor unsuspecting new doctor was prepared for his newest patient, the daughter from hell.

The idea of finally dumping my unwanted endometrial companion motivated uncharacteristic promptness. I arrived for the appointment not just on time, but early. Upon arrival, I was taken straight into the doctor's office where, like a good patient, I waited patiently.

I had encountered this man only once briefly the previous year, after he successfully renovated my mother's plumbing by repairing a leaky faucet. After a few days of playing nursemaid to my mother, I was in no mood for formal introductions or conversations with anyone, especially not the very person responsible for mom's irascible, bedridden disposition.

Just six months later and here I was cooling my own heels in his office, waiting to personally present him with the good news. He was to have the opportunity to cut on yet another female family member. Two within a year, a mother-daughter surgical patient duo would be a record for us. It had to be a record for him, too. When it was all said and done, we were surely a family he would not soon forget.

I sat alone in his office waiting, just the sound of a nearby clock keeping me company. Each ticking sound was a reminder of a moment gone by, another minute minus the main character in this plot. He was late, and it was Friday afternoon.

Patience is not a virtue I was blessed with. When God handed out that trait, I thought He said patients. Haunted with precognition of medical mayhem, I ran to the back of the line. So here I sat cooling my heels, tapping my fingers, checking out the good doc's decor, and wondering if I was doing the right thing. Out of sheer boredom I inspected the diploma's proudly displayed on every wall.

For entertainment I decided to try my hand at guessing his age. A true sign I was indeed getting older! I calculated the years since he graduated from each of his institutions, college, medical school, and the completion of his internship. I added, subtracted, and then added some more. However, the figures didn't seem to add up. Something had to be wrong. Maybe my math was off, or I was wrong about the years, this year or the year he graduated. I tried the math a second time. Once the tally was taken, the results remained. No way, something had to be terribly awry.

Again the counting commenced, but this time I wouldn't rely solely on my head for all the calculations. I would employ the use of my fingers and toes. No, that wouldn't really work; I had shoes on. I checked the diploma's again, this time looking closer. The numbers were correct, but there was no way I would accept the outcome. The man I was about to solicit to cut on me was younger than me. That seemed utterly impossible. Could I, should I, allow a mere child to chisel away on my antique anatomy?

Doubt and worry engulfed me as images of a young and green Dr. Frankenstein, testing his newly learned and yet-to-be-tried methods on me, crept into my overimaginative mind. The door was calling and I was about to bolt when who strolled in but the youngster himself. Immediately I looked to his chin and cheeks to determine if he was old enough to shave. Whoa! My fears calmed as he was adorned with not only fuzz, but a full beard. At least he had passed the puberty-prong test. Maybe he could perform the chore at hand.

Bearing the Big H

Who was I fooling? I was desperate; and this was the best of my options, family-tested, tried and true. My mother had stood as his (and now my) guinea pig. She lived and so would I, hopefully. My preoccupation with his age gave way to the purpose of my visit, my request, and reason for being there. Dispelling the generation gap, I broached the subject, seized the moment and let "Dr. Doogie Houser" have it.

Because I was sick and tired, mainly tired of being sick from being a total woman, I made my unconditional demands of surrender known. No time was wasted in getting down to the purpose of this visit. Nothing was left to his imagination as I poured and puked my vile rendition of my condition to the physician.

I caught him quite off guard. The poor man had barely dispensed with the formality of introducing himself when the verbal barrage began.

"I want to become a eunuchette and I have chosen you to do the honors. If you can't or won't do that, then at least give me a sex change operation," I continued without catching my breath. "I have chosen you as the person I want to remove my female organs and with it this pest which is wrecking havoc on my home life. I don't want to do this anymore. I don't want to *be* this anymore!"

I paused only for air. I wasn't quite through driving home the fact that I was totally finished with *complete* woman-hood. I had vowed that by the time my speech was over, he would understand, completely and unconditionally, without any doubt what I wanted and what I demanded!

While I equipped myself with enough breath to conclude my spiel, the good doc took the liberty of picking his jaw up off the floor. Once I ceased verbally relieving myself, the man showed no reluctance to my demands. Whether it was the way I was digging my fingernails into his wooden chair as I spoke, or the veins protruding through my beet-red forehead, or the bulging eyeballs, I don't know but I got the feeling he felt threatened, or at least intimidated.

Given my history, it didn't take a rocket scientist to know that a hysterectomy was the proper course of action. Upon hearing a condensed version of my gynecological problems over the past twenty years, he agreed that the time was right for me to take the big step and undergo the Big H.

Normally I would have been full of questions, weighing the pros and cons. Not this time, not this surgery. I had tried all of my other options, with less than satisfactory results. It was time for total eradication, total removal, and total annihilation of all that that literally haunted me on an all-too-routine, biweekly basis.

Right then and there my doctor and I scheduled my "Big H." We discussed all that was medically required, the ins and outs of the surgery. He dutifully listed all those legally required possibilities and potential pitfalls of his pending performance, the gamut that ranged from minor to major, plumbing problems to paralysis, and even death.

From my past professional legal experience, I knew that the laundry list was not intended to scare a possible victim; it was required for physician protection in case he messed up my body, I got mad and tried to sue. I was already screwed up and was now ready to be relieved, regardless of the risk. As soon as his pitch was over, we scheduled the removal of my female organs for May 6 of the thirty-eighth year of my life.

I thought this office visit would be just that, an "office" visit. Little did I know an encounter with the table and stirrups was also to be part of the routine. It was only as I got up to leave the doc's office that the full extent of this visit was discovered. As I began to head toward the door, the outer office, the exit, I felt strong, masculine, medical hands gripping my shoulders steering me in the opposite direction, down the hall, toward the examining room. Quickly I grabbed the door frame, dug my heels in and held on for dear life. Why I wondered, did he have to see anything now when soon he would be getting a bird's-eye view, an extremely up-close internal view.

"Where are we going?" I asked with a dread-filled crackling voice. As if I didn't know the answer to that rhetorical question. "What are you doing? What do you need to know now that you won't discover in a few weeks? Is this completely necessary?"

Why I wondered, did he have to see anything now when soon he would be getting a bird's-eye view, an extremely up-close, extremely internal view.

Allow me to explain one thing here. I am not a chicken. I know the drill, all too well. During my years of feminine physical exams, I had become accustomed to the annual poking and prodding routine-as accustomed as any woman possibly could be with her back to the table, her raised feet strung out before her, strategically placed in funky metal holsters, and her legs wide-open and stretched across an area the width of the Grand Canyon. Then I'm expected to lay perfectly still while some strange person inserts cold things in a way, and to a depth, that no man has ever traveled before. Oh yeah. I was always anxious to get in that position and have that done— and then actually pay for the experience. When you think about the whole thing, it's worse than a trip to the dentist, far more unnerving than nails across a blackboard. So I DON'T think of it. Once a year I just take the position, cop the Nike attitude and *Just Do It*. But I had my dose this year. As far as I was concerned, I'd had enough for the next decade.

Resistance has never been part of my ritual, so I was surprised at my reluctance this time. But then, there was a plausible explanation for me standing in the hallway stuttering and stammering, arguing with my doctor over the true necessity of the impending pelvic prodding.

Like so many other things in life, it all had to do with age. (The older we get, the more things seem to correlate to age.) One problem with getting older is that doctors either truly become younger or get younger looking. Either way, it is not a wrinkle-soothing formula. Unfortunately, not only was the one before me younger, he was also younger looking—and good-looking, as well.

One of the few things I had not encountered in all my years of gynecological warfare was the fate of having a cute, young ob-gyn, the kind that, given any other circumstances, would cause my head to turn and my hormones to kick in to overdrive. I prefer older, balding, heavyset, unattractive doctors peering at my private parts. Why I did something as dumb as selecting a handsome doctor this time is a mystery to me. Maybe I was certain that this would be the last hurrah, the last voyage to the bottom of the "V." Maybe it was because I was older. Or was it that I was no longer an old maid but now an old married woman? Well, I reasoned, if mom can overlook it, so can I.

Whatever my reasoning, it was wrong. For the first time in twenty years I was embarrassed, flustered, and my cheeks (the two above my neck) actually turned a rosy shade of pink during the exam. Get a load of that. At my age, after all I had encountered, and now a physical exam made my skin color change in a way that would have made a chameleon jealous. This was a new one on me. Believe it or not, I am not shy. Never have been. That is an adjective that has never, ever been used in conjunction with or seen anywhere near my name, first or last.

The only good news is that the doctor had his head at the opposite end of that which was color-coded. Unless my bottom blushed too, my secret was safe. And although this strong, bold and brazen woman was transformed into a wimpish prude, the preoperative physical exam went off without a hitch. Before departing the office and allowing the young doctor the opportunity to resume his peaceful practice, I couldn't resist one last zesty zinger.

"Do you realize how many doctors I had to select from, and what an honor it is that I have chosen you for this mission of mercy?" I asked with a straight face. "I think as a token of this encounter you should consider putting my organs in a glass jar to sit proudly on your fireplace mantel as a constant reminder of the honor that has been bestowed upon you." He simply smiled. He didn't agree. He didn't refuse.

With all the physical prerequisites behind me, I was ready to proceed to the next level of preparation, the mental portion. This, fortunately, was a private examination: One with and by me, myself and I, conducted in the privacy of my car. My husband had offered to accompany me on this doctor's visit, but I had refused his kindness. I wanted to make the journey alone, mainly because of the hour and a half of quiet time the drive would provide. This was no small deal. I was about to undergo a life-altering, major surgery and, despite my humor, jokes, and eagerness, I realized that. As I had known it would, the full realization kicked in on that long, lonely drive home.

Bearing the Big H

New subjects for worry were just what my idle mind had needed. With the Big H now set and looming overhead, my mind went into high gear and the race was on. During that boring drive home, nothing was spared. It was an emotional frenzy. Imagine experiencing the whole emotional spectrum from fear, sadness to relief, remorse, and reluctance in the amount of time it takes to wash a load of laundry. The ride on this emotional roller coaster was one of the wildest I had ever experienced, even scarier-and bumpier-than the PMS misery-go-round ride. It was a miracle I was able to maneuver the car with the turbulent psychotic trip my mind was taking.

True to character, my biggest emotion was guilt. I always feel guilty, about everything. My counselor says I should entirely eliminate the word from my vocabulary and replace it with the word *responsible*. According to her, guilt denotes the necessity for punishment. I tried following her advice, but I felt guilty about being responsible all the time, for everything and to everyone. Besides that, it just doesn't sound the same, doesn't pack the same punch. I don't think the statement, "I feel responsible for eating that gallon of ice cream last week," portrays the same dramatic and traumatic tone.

Whichever way I phrased it, the impending procedure weighed heavily on my shoulders. After sharing my internal organs for almost two decades with my constant trespassing companion, I felt guilty for taking the money, the time, and the risk for major surgery. I somehow viewed this hysterectomy, an "elective" surgery. At times I felt my twisted mind attempting to convince me this was not a remedy I was entitled to, but a luxury I was not worthy of. Oh, would my therapist love to get a hold of that statement—as well as me for making it!

With each mile I drove, the guilt snowballed. By the time I arrived home, this loving wife my husband is accustomed to was lost to some guilt-consumed lunatic. And my unsuspecting mate made a fatal error. Being an engineer, he was eager to collect the pertinent data and he did so without first checking the wife's temperament gauge. The door wasn't even completely closed when my caring and adoring darling of a spouse began his line of questioning.

"How was your appointment Dear? The doctor, did you

like him? What did he say? Did he suggest surgery?"

"I can't, I just can't do it!" I cried. "It is too costly. I just had surgery. It's too time-consuming, too long of a hospital stay. I will be out of commission too long. Who will cook for you, clean house, do the laundry, and walk the dogs? I can't subject you and everyone else to this foolishness."

I must admit it took a good long time and the skills of a patient, intelligent, and cunning man to calm me down and sort out the facts from fiction. After a hair-raising, seminervous breakdown, we had a heart-to-heart discussion, at which time my rational other half helped convince this irrational half (wit) that the surgery was more than just needed, it was necessary—and after that display, more now than ever.

The following week, it was all made official with a pre-operative visit to the hospital. There I had a small dose of what awaited: needles, needles, and more needles. They took blood for typing; they took blood for testing. They even took blood to determine how I bleed. Vials and vials of blood, so much blood there had to be enough for an all-you-can-eat buffet for bats.

Yet it all was going quite smoothly. My emotions were under control. I had been convinced there was nothing to worry about as far as the surgery was concerned. There was just one small thing that concerned me. Keeping secret the nature of my surgery. With the operation fast approaching, that seemed to become a priority.

Living in a city the size of ours, gossip is not just a way of life, but for some it *is* their life. On any given day of the week, one can venture into the local donut shop, café, or grocery store to catch up on most anyone's personal life. The bigger the problem, the juicier the gossip, the more coveted the contents. The local rumor mill in our city is like an ice-cream parlor in larger towns. Instead of flavors of the week, we have rumors of the week. I was from a large metropolitan area where residents were one among the millions. It was a place where neighbors lived next to neighbors without knowing (or caring to know) the name or number of those living next door. I had come from that to this.

No one, nothing, was immune from the town rumor mill. There is even a club in town appropriately called

"Tippers." Members of this elite group converge at the weekly hot spot, drink coffee, and have a contest to see who has the best gossip of the week. The one who lays claim to the best tip of the week gets the dubious honor of paying the tab for everyone's coffee. Only here in our small city would one find a social club for dispelling gossip in such a fashionable manner.

I did not relish the thought of my impending surgery being the subject of the week's news flash. I was, after all, about to lose my womanhood, or at least those organs that were integral to being a woman, that which literally and physically distinguishes me from a man—*w* for womb and *o* for ovaries.

I managed to swear my husband to silence. He promised, at the risk of death, not to disclose the objective of my operation. It would be a secret surgery. That was it. All the obstacles, the last of my excuses, had been overcome. There was nothing remaining and I had no option but to be brave and go forward.

"Onward and out with my organs!" was my cheer. I was ready to go on, take the next step and show up for the date with my surgeon and his handy-dandy scalpel. Then it hit me. I was about to be among an elite group of women referred to as surgically menopausal. Oh, what status awaited me! I was ready, willing, and so eager to lay claim to my new title and all its perks. The closer the surgery, the more my fantasies and dreams mushroomed. I was riding high, ready for all that lay before me. All, that is, except the meddling.

Despite my best efforts, it didn't take long for word to spread that I was about to have an operation. I was the city reporter for the only city newspaper, and was prematurely retiring on the pretense of an impending medical undertaking.

As previously mentioned, I live in a close, *very* close-knit community. It wasn't long before the inquiring minds wanted to know—more. When asked, I would only say it was female surgery. That would quiet the men. The women, on the other hand, found that response an open invitation to share all their womanly woes. At my tender age I never dreamed anyone would correctly guess the type of surgery I was having. However, two women hit the nail on the head. To add insult to injury, they didn't even have the courtesy to ask point-blank if they were correct in their assumptions. They just yakked on, continuing in their conversation as if they *knew* they were correct. The audacity.

The first wise woman took me totally by surprise, as she blatantly carried on a monologue, with me by her side. Nonchalantly she described her personal experience, which I knew nothing about and cared less to know. According to her rendition, what I was about to undergo was just a day at the beach.

"I hear you are retiring,"she said as we stood among a crowd gathered for a public event.

"Yes, I am." I did not know her well, and we had barely spoken to one another the past few years.

"What are you going to do with all your time?" she inquired.

"Well, first I am having surgery, and recuperation will take time, so I have been told," I answered smoothly, with a little secrecy, but cool enough not to provoke further inquiry.

"Oh, I had that same surgery just last year, and you'll feel so much better afterwards. The only regret I had was not having it sooner. Just one piece of advice though," she rambled on without coming up for air. "Don't do what I did and get up too soon because you will regret it later. About the fourth week you will start to really feel better, and by that time you will be bored out of your wits and ready to venture out. But beware. I did that and went back to work, then had a relapse that set me back several weeks."

Without even seeking a confirmation from me, she then proceeded to dispense more unsolicited advice.

"So take your time getting out and about," she concluded with a conspiratorial smile that only a veteran could muster.

So dumbfounded by her accuracy, and boldness that I actually only heard every other word that came out of her know-it-all mouth.

She couldn't possibly know that I was about to embark on the Big H, could she? My mind went into overdrive and paranoia once again set in. It was my husband. He had talked, broken his vow of silence. I would cut his tongue from his hard head and nail it to a tree outside our kitchen window for him to see every day as he gummed his breakfast down.

Before I began wielding my double-edged sword (you can bet your sweet bippy it's a large, serrated number) on him, I decided I'd better make certain of the facts. Reluctantly, I went back to the one whom had said so much and conveyed so little. Before I confronted my other half and made him just a quarter, I needed to ascertain her source of information. She might or might not be able to spare my husband and his oh-so-useful tongue.

"How did you know what kind of surgery I was having?" I asked her nervously. "Where did you hear it? Did someone tell you? Was it my husband?"

"No one told me, and I have heard nothing. I just assumed, having been through it, and you being a woman, and at your age. How old are you, anyway? Aren't you kind of young to be having a hysterectomy?"

The nerve of that woman. How dare she guess the object of my delicate secret. My paranoia returned to the scene. Now it would be all over town, possibly the state and maybe even the nation. She was, after all, the local director of tourism! Forget overdrive, my imagination was now throttling down in four-wheel drive. Her newest tourist-enticing telephone conversation played in my mind.

"Yes, this is a wonderful city, full of historical sites, beautiful city parks, and two lakes. If you hurry and visit soon, and if you are lucky, you might even catch a glimpse of our local eunuchette as she comes home from the hospital, minus her female organs of course," she'd mimic into the telephone to inquiring tourists.

Visitors and locales alike would get involved in the action. The hotels would book quickly. Bookies would get rich taking bets on my temperament.

"I bet twenty that she is more of a witch afterwards than she was before she went in."

"I'll wager thirty that she and her husband will split within three months of her being on her back unable to do anything but bark commands."

"Ten says she is up, out of retirement and back to work within six weeks."

How could I disappoint the entire town? I had no choice

but to go through with surgery now that tourists would be coming and the wagering had begun. Surely I'd made the big time and become the "Tipper" topic of the week. How many could brag of that star-studded status?

At any rate, it took only a few more conversations with women for me to realize the past decade had dramatically changed the attitude regarding the Big H. It was not the big deal it once was.

According to some postoperative patients, the hysterectomy is no longer a surgery reserved for dire cases. No longer is it considered solely an operation of last resort. No longer is it frowned upon as an option. No longer are women forced to endure the pain of womanhood past childbearing. Nor are women forced to reckon with the lingering wrath of *Mommy* Nature *Dearest*. I learned too that, in this day and age, a hysterectomy is no longer taboo, nor shrouded in a veil of secrecy.

Darn those changing times and surgical advancements. Now I was disappointed. How would I be unique if only one of many? I envisioned my impending new "surgically menopausal" status as elite. Would I not be considered a novelty? This late in my life would I actually be doing something viewed as normal? Nah, not me! Never!

THREE

Hystery In
The Making

Admittedly I went to extremes in preparing for surgery. I had a luxury not many people have when getting ready to go under the knife. I quit my job. Okay, the long recovery was a good excuse, but it wasn't the sole reason for my early retirement though it sounded good. I'm telling you, I took advantage of this whole surgery routine and milked it for all it was worth. And it was definitely worth being worthless, if only for a while.

Part of milking it to the max was maneuvering my early retirement to have some free time before the surgery. After all, I was about to embark on major surgery and endure a long recovery, which meant I was deserving of quality time before the big day, the big deed. Therefore, I quit my job several weeks beforehand to ensure ample time to play, time to prepare, and then some more play time.

Oh, how glorious that first day of total freedom! I got up late and drank coffee for a long time. I sat on the patio leisurely listening to the birds sing and watching the grass grow. How sweet—and short—it was. Before I knew it, the days had dwindled down to just tee minus one and counting.

I spent the last of my intact time, the day before surgery, with my husband. He had taken the day off to be with me and calm my rapidly unraveling nerves. We opted for an outing that would allow me to vent my fear by swinging a big club at something intended to be hit. So off to the golf course we went. As I swung the club, my husband carefully kept his eye on the unpredictable direction of both the ball and the golf club. He was intent on staying out of my line of fire.

Although my golf game left much to be desired, it was a real blessing in disguise. As happens every month to fertile types, I was ovulating that day. The pain, just from the release of a few eggs, was so intense and overwhelming I was forced, after only a hole or two, to put my club down and become merely a cart chauffeur. This was another fine example of Mother Nature's sick sense of humor. One more jab before the jabbing was all over. She had to stick it to me one final time, and she waited until the last hour to bid me farewell, in a manner only she could manage.

Right then, on the number two fairway, I found myself actually counting the hours, anxiously awaiting the relief operation. I wanted it all to go away and for some degree of normalcy (if it ever existed) to return to my life. At that moment, had the doctor been playing with us, I would have pleaded for him to make a hole in one desperate woman, immediately.

I was no longer apprehensive about the surgery. On the contrary I was quite relaxed about it all. It's amazing what a little round of golf with Mother Nature can do for one's disposition. It had a way of dispelling all lingering apprehension. With the fear and worry out of the way, I slept like a baby the night before surgery.

While I was peacefully snoozing, something happened. A new day arrived. But this was not just any day. It was the day, and I was up and at it early (a real understatement). Nothing stood between me and eradication but a few short hours and a long drive. The hospital was 40 miles away and I had to be at the hospital at 6 a.m. which meant we had to be on the road by five o'clock in the morning. So I was up at 4:30 a.m. With makeup, fingernail polish, and all the other necessities of life prohibited, I didn't need time to do anything but shower and get my butt in the car.

I will be completely honest here and admit I'm not a morning person. I like my sleep and it likes me. During my teenage years, I learned to claim the need for beauty sleep, although the benefits were somewhat questionable upon the face of a pimple-prone pubescent. Then, as now, given the opportunity, I can sleep for hours upon hours. In the few weeks between my last day on the job and my newfound freedom, I had quickly fallen victim to old habits. I confess I even fibbed to my husband on a few occasions when he inquired as to the time of my arising. (The guilt made me do it).

"When are you getting up?" my employed mate would query as he left for work.

"I'm getting up now and getting busy," impressively I replied. Once the coast was clear, I'd lumber back to bed and slumber until my body tired of inactivity.

Though I prefer to sleep in, I am not opposed to an early rise once in awhile, but this surgery required taking early to the extreme. It was predawn. I had to wake before the rooster sounded, before the dark gave way to dawn, before Mister Sun kissed the horizon and bid the darkness good-bye. I was surprised to find my alarm clock could even be set for such an outrageous time!

At the time of scheduling, I halfheartedly insisted on a later surgery time. Though I knew it was a futile effort, at least I let my preference be known. They had their reasons for making me arrive so early; I was certain it was for more presurgery sticking and pricking, poking, and prodding. I was right. By the time they finished and wheeled me in to the operating room, I really did feel sick. All those preliminary procedures have a way of turning even the healthiest into sickly types.

For the life of me, I can't figure out why if a person hasn't had anything to eat or drink twelve hours prior to surgery, it's necessary for a cleansing, of the internal type. There is no other way to say this other than to just blurt it out. I hate enemas! To me they are one of the worst parts of any surgery. They are nasty and make a person do natural things unnaturally. I don't like the squirt, and I really don't like the magnitude and manner in which the squirt does its job. However, on this particular occasion it was not the enema as much as the other cleansing tool that took its toll on me.

At the time of check-in I was taken to a very nice room and told to relax, the nurse would be in soon. How does one relax while wondering what merriment awaits? It wasn't the looming surgery that caused me worry. It was all the stuff that stood between the operating table and me. As if on cue, the nurse entered the room. And boy, was she ever loaded down. She was armed with internal cleansing instruments of all types. In one hand she carried an enema, and in the other was that little bottle bound for the other opening.

As a baby boomer, I have the dubious distinction of being raised during the disposable days. From cigarette lighters to disposable plates, cups, and utensils, it seems as if everything these days is disposable. I remember when wash and reuse was the way of life. Now there are throwaway this and throwaway that; everything is use and then into the refuse. No wonder our landfills runneth over.

This new era ushered in some contents for conflict. Used to be kids made extra money collecting soda pop bottles and turning them in for the nickel refund. That was before plastic replaced glass and forced young weekend entrepreneurs into bankruptcy. Then there is the disposable diaper dilemma. While considered a wonderful invention and a godsend by many moms, my dear old dad cursed their very existence. Dad was a traveling salesman, and it never failed that while driving the highways and byways a diaper or two would litter the landscape. The disgusting sight always prompted the same response from dad, "Those damn disposable diapers are the devil's own invention."

Then, of course, there is an exhaustive line of disposable feminine products. There is the disposable tampon applicator, located on the grocery shelf near various brands of disposable douche. The little throwaway, squeeze bottle is the only douche container I had known. But, there was a time . . .

As a young child—a nosy young child—I liked to explore and snoop. One day while exploring in the "no child zone" better known as my parent's bathroom, I stumbled across something I had never seen before. It was a strange, ugly, rubber contraption hidden behind the closet door, just hanging on a hook out of sight and out of mind to most. Being an inquisitive child, I stood, stared, and wondered about this weird thing. But puzzled I would remain, for I knew better than to inquire about something located off limits to me. It was many years later that I finally linked the teenage term *douche bag* with the ominous object from the past.

Well, it was the disposable age combined with my lack of schooling in the old-fashioned ways that came back to haunt me now, during these preoperative procedures.

The nurse needed to ask only once, and I very obediently took her medical supplies and headed for the bathroom. I didn't want her assistance in my assignment.

In the bathroom the first big dilemma was deciding which one to deliver first. It didn't really matter, as it was all to come out in the wash. The enema won and with little fanfare was dispensed in the proper manner. Next was the douche. Now, had this been the kind I was accustomed to, there would have been nothing to cuss or discuss. But no, this resembled that novelty which many years before had perplexed my pea brain. Now, here I was face to face with the same designer bag. As instructed I filled it with warm water, hung it *up* on the hook so it would flow, and inserted the nozzle into the appropriate opening.

I waited but felt nothing. I waited some more and still did not feel my female parts filling with warm liquid. So being an impatient and quick-fixing person, I pulled the plug. As soon as I did, the unthinkable happened. Dark yellowish-orange liquid sprayed forth in a fashion and with a gusto that made Old Faithful seem like a dud. I tried to catch the hose, but my eyes were blinded by the Betadine solution that was soaking me and my wonderful hospital apparel to the bones. Nothing in that small cubbyhole was spared the wrath of that spit-fired sprayer. The walls were decorated with abstract art, a bright color and a wild design. I screamed and then laughed, as I attempted to tackle the tube. Finally I wrestled the squirter under control and crimped its neck, sending the sprayer down toward the floor in total defeat. However, the damage had been done. From the toilet seat to the sink, floor to ceiling, and wall to wall, not an inch was spared the splattering of the douche bag decor.

With nurse and husband waiting on the other side of the door, I quickly got to work erasing all the artwork that adorned the bathroom. Besides discovering a new art technique, the real positive was that all the cleansing solution was on the walls, so there was none left to be shot inward and upward into this new, yet to be discovered artist.

Was this to set the tone of my day? Oh, what would I encounter next? From here it had to be all downhill. With these necessities dispensed with, it was time to get started and set the gurney in motion. First I had to change my attire, again. The nurse had me remove my hospital blues and then decked me out in the latest of hospital fashions, a new style that consisted of a funky, newfangled, silver, thermal shower cap and matching metallic leggings. Reflecting the fluorescent lights and shining in silver, I looked like something out of a sci-fi film. It was explained to me that these new duds were not just a fashion statement but served a real purpose; namely to ensure warmth while patients were cooling their heels in the walk-in cooler also known as the operating room. All dressed up in my new outfit, I was finally ready. With my spouse beside me and the nurse pushing my gurney, off we went. The silver bullet with her sidekicks in tow, we were surgery bound.

After waiting all morning, once downstairs in the pre-operative station, I was wheeled into a curtain-covered cubicle, only to wait some more. It seemed something was missing. Oh yeah, it was the doctor. My surgery was scheduled for 7:30 and here it was 7:20 and I hadn't seen hide or hair of him. And I wasn't the only one. My overly large and conversation-sensitive ears just happened to overhear the nurses talking about (or rather questioning) the doctor's whereabouts, and wondering outloud why he was so late. That did little to calm my already crabby disposition.

Then, as if appearing out of thin air, voila, he was there. Late but there. When he finally waltzed in, it was not to a warm welcome from me. As hard as I tried, I was unable to contain my curt tongue. Dumb, dumb, dumb! He was after all the person that, in just a few short minutes, would be cutting and carving, holding my very life in his hands.

Nevertheless, my mouth was like a runaway steam engine barreling out of control, bound for the surgeon before me. As I rambled, he scrambled to finish tying a knot in his scrubs.

"It's too early and too dark outside for golf, so I suppose you stopped off for coffee before coming by here. I am so glad you decided to grace us with your presence. Nothing like waiting to the last moment. I hope I haven't inconvenienced you this morning. Should I come back at a more opportune time?" I quizzed him from the gurney. With my mouth still in motion the nurses quickly wheeled me past him and into the operating room.

In addition to taping the IV to my hand, they should have applied some of that adhesive material to the big, wide, gaping hole located just beneath my nose.

Of course, my behavior (or lack of) always comes equipped with an excuse. This time was no exception and this time I had a real dozy. I was under the influence of some kind of drug they were pumping into my system at the precise moment I was mumbling. That had to be it because, while I am a blonde, I am not dumb enough to aggravate a surgeon about to be armed with a scalpel aimed at my abdomen.

Evidentially I didn't ruffle his scrubs too badly because the surgery went well, as far as I know. I was out of it and I knew nothing until I awoke to the face of my cute little doctor hovering over me in the recovery room. My first question was the one that, despite the number of surgeries, remained the same.

"Was there any endometriosis?"

I faintly remember him saying there was a great deal.

The conversation went straight south from there. I don't recall much about my recovery room experience with the doctor, and that which I do remember I'd like to forget. It is important to keep in mind here the fact I was heavily sedated, under the influence of *major* drugs, not of sound mind, and certainly not in my right mind when I opened my mouth to speak to him this time.

Although groggy I remember confessing to my own doctor that I had actually been horny the night before. I don't know what got in to me. Me, of all people, actually being in the desire mode and then admitting it. How unlikely it all seemed. Maybe it was in anticipation of being without and unable. It's human nature to want what you cannot have. I never remember craving sex. The only thing resembling horny in my entire life involved a wild chase through the woods. And then those cool, four-legged elusive reptile critters always managed to escape the confines of my childhood grasps. My horniness is as rare as finding a horny toad these days. Like my sexual drive, they are in danger of extinction.

However, horny and its definition are not the point here. What's important and oh-so-appalling is that I actually conveyed my wanton desires to another human being, a man, a near stranger, and my gynecologist at that! Oh, the things we mutter when coming out of anesthesia. I will never know, nor do I ever want to know, whether I was bragging or, in my sedative state, thought the recovery room a confessional and my gynecologist a priest. (Yeah, right).

I have tried very hard since that moment to forget the entire conversation, to completely block it out of my mind. The thought of it makes this conservative and modest woman go crazy. And it gets even worse. The candid chatter took a downward dive after that confession. To make even a bigger fool out of myself, I then proceeded to reveal the contents of a steamy dream I had about the two of us (unfortunately, yes, us as in me and my gynecologist) sitting in a sand trap together. The saving grace here is that somehow I managed to permanently eliminate from my memory bank all that was said from that point forward. Repression can be a good thing.

It was bad enough I actually had a dream about my gynecologist, but then to blurt out the contents to him was even worse. Now I know why I always prefer ugly gynecologists. This had never happened before. Of course, I blame him for being in the recovery room where he had no business being, much less conversing with a woman under the influence, and totally out of her mind.

That is what I like about myself. When I do things, I do them right. I was born in Texas, where everything is big. So naturally when I make an ass out of myself, I do it in a big, really big way

Once my severe case of diarrhea of the mouth was over, the remainder of my hospital stay was rather uneventful. Probably because I was drugged and comatose, just the way the nursing staff likes a patient.

I would not rate my accommodations as four-star, but what was lacking in food was found in drugs. To ensure the quality of my stay, I was provided with what is routinely referred to in the medical world as a P.C.A. pump. My doctor personally defines this as a device used after surgery to blunt the pain caused by an unfeeling surgeon. To the patient it is a wonderful thing, used to kill the pain before you are even aware of the pain. It's a self-medicating tool intended to keep a patient pain free and less of a pain in the butt to the nurses. With the P.C.A. pump connected to the bed and at hand, there is no need to call a nurse every time pain disturbs the drug-induced slumber.

I think it is a tool used by family and friends, as well as medical staff, to guarantee all patients are good patients. If I was not personally pushing the pump and self-medicating, my husband was pushing the drugs on me and for me. Although it was against the rules, he would occasionally step in and do the pumping. However, my spouse knows oh too well the degree of my stubbornness and how I dislike dispensing medication into my thick-skinned body. In an attempt to circumvent the tough-girl routine and prevent unnecessary pain, he took it upon himself to man the button when I was refusing.

My surgery was on a Thursday, routinely my doctor's day off. I was certain there was a connection between the predawn surgery schedule and the awaiting golf links. I have the feeling my doctor decided on medical school only after he failed to make the PGA cut. With sunny skies and warm, spring days, I did not see him after the recovery room rendezvous, which was a blessing. His associate checked on me in the evening. From that conversation I gathered he had indeed managed to make the golf course after he finished de-wombing me.

It was not until the next day, when he managed to find the time to actually visit me that I discovered out how important golf really was to him. Not only was he playing a round after my operation, he was in a tournament. However, he did credit his placing in that contest with having cut on me. Was he insinuating there was a link between performing a hysterectomy and playing a good round of golf?

After we finished discussing these important issues, we got to my surgery and my recovery. He went over the rules of recovery: no lifting, no strenuous activities, and most importantly, no sex for at least six weeks. Wow! Wonderful! No need for the headache routine for a while. I could dispense with the aspirin. Then he proceeded to explain what he had encountered when he opened me up. What he had found, I had never heard of.

"Not only was there a large amount of endometriosis, but there was a chocolate cyst."

"A chocolate *what?*" I countered.

"You heard it right, a chocolate cyst. It is a mass that oozes a thick chocolate-syrup-type liquid when popped."

How lovely the image. A chocolate cyst. Where in the world do these doctors come up with such terms? How could they do such a horrible injustice? What would prompt the medical profession to name a disgusting, dark brown growth after something as delightful and delicious as chocolate? It was definitely an oxymoron. Chocolate is a woman's best friend. It is something so edible, incredible, delectable, and oh-so-sinful. Chocolate is what I crave at least once a month, if you know what I mean. A cyst, on the other hand, is the dreaded enemy, a beast whose existence is centered on and around tormenting women world-wide.

This tidbit of information was certainly not something I would broadcast to my friends when they inquired as to the success of my surgery. This chocolate cyst stuff would go no further; it would be sealed within the confines of my medical records and protected by the doctor-patient privilege. This secret would go to the grave with me. While it was disgusting enough to be considered top secret, classified information, it wasn't enough to faze my chocolate fetish.

FOUR

The Walking Wounded

By far the biggest challenge during my venture at the hospital hotel came on the second day of my stay. Oddly enough it too, occurred in the bathroom. The incident, by most female standards, was borderline criminal; it should rank right up there with irreconcilable differences and mental anguish as grounds for divorce. From the very start, it promised to be a day I would never forget.

The medical staff wasted no time in making certain I could, and, would, walk again after surgery. They wanted me up and at 'em and made no bones about it. There was even a well-thought-out plan of action about to be unleashed upon this unsuspecting patient. Because I was so naïve and so drugged, it took time for me to recognize the method to their madness.

The whole saga began a mere twenty-three hours after the Big H when a solemn-looking nurse awakened me. She had this alarming smile—an impish grin—one so startling it sent chills up my spine, and made me brace for the worse.

"It is time to take out your catheter," she chirped cheerfully, though quietly. I am sure she didn't want to disturb my husband soundly sleeping in a nearby recliner. It was, after all, only six in the morning.

I couldn't believe the nerve of that man. During all the commotion, my husband never stirred nor broke his rhythmic snore. I was amazed, as well as somewhat peeved, that his sounds of slumber were allowed to continue roaring as my temporary tinkling tube was removed. However, the all-too-familiar husbandly tunes did manage to make me feel right at home while the nurse did her duty.

Back to the scheme at hand. I had it all figured out, the real reason they wanted to pull my plug so soon after surgery. The nurse wanted me up, to actually move my body, and butt, out of bed. What better incentive than the relentless urge of the bladder? Therein lay their sneaky strategy; that nice little nurse wanted to take my tube as a means of motivation. With no catheter or bedpan in sight, I would eventually have to putter to pee.

Now, I was *told* a little different story. My nurse said the catheter was removed to make certain the bladder functioned properly. Yeah right!

"It's standard procedure and required before a patient can be discharged," she cunningly cooed.

But I knew better. She was testing the old carrot-in-front-of-the-horse theory. I'm no dummy; I knew the real reason she was so anxious to yank my tank. Do you think I would voluntarily leave my pain-free position in the safety of my soft bed? No way, I was comfy and resting soundly (though not as soundly as my husband!) But what could I do? What were my options? Stay in bed and water my surroundings?

No more stalling was to be had. Although waiting patiently the nurse was, nevertheless, waiting. There was no way around it. The time had come to dispense with my dispenser. Clutching the tube tightly (a little less tightly than my jaw was clinched) she began. So swift her yank I hardly noticed the removal of my portable plumbing. To my utter surprise, the dispensing of my bedside pouch was relatively painless. Of course, everything *is* relative.

With that detail out of the way, I had no choice but to move. Cleverly I had been suckered into making the trip to the powder room, which of course, was strategically located *across* the room. The next time I had to tinkle it would be time to teeter. The nurse left me to contemplate not my navel, but my kidneys.

It took awhile, but their plan eventually worked. Oh, the power of suggestion. The urge soon arrived and I knew it was time to take care of the bladder matter. So reluctantly I rang for the nurse. She knew full well what was needed. Within minutes she was back at my bedside, positioning me for my maiden voyage.

In all the ruckus, *Sleeping Beauty* awoke. From the the deepening of my worry lines, he could detect I was about to undertake a major move. He rose to his feet and fled to my side. Strategically he positioned himself, staying out of my way, yet close enough to catch me on the first bounce, if need be.

It was such a sight to behold. There the two of them stood, he with his *Pitiful Pearl* of an expression and the optimistic nurse coaxing and coaching all the while. She gave an instructional barrage as to the finer (and less painful) points of how best to maneuver outward and onward without busting my belly open. Having received detailed walking orders, I prepared to tackle the toilet trail.

In anticipation of this momentous occasion, a swing set, complete with trapeze, had been erected onto the bed and hovered above my head. I tried as long as I could to procrastinate, find an excuse to keep from having to use the grip. The mere thought of pulling myself *up* with my recently tortured tummy sent chills over my body. Soon I became paralyzed with fear. I even tried that as an excuse. However, the nurse would not budge. She just waited and watched, tapping her toes and pacing the floor. I knew the only way I would ever find peace was to appease her.

I began to pray my pain pills would carry me through. I had stalled enough. The time had come; there was no way around it. I had a courageous plan. In one swift motion I would pull myself up, turn a full forty-five degrees, and then swing both legs over the side of the bed before a rest. There was only one way this would work, quickly. I had to do it all in one fatal swoop, without time to think about what I was doing.

Do it and suffer afterwards, was my thought. I took one deep, deep breath, "One, two, three . . ." Then with all the strength—and nerve—I could muster, my upward motion began. Quickly I reached overhead for the trapeze. Tightly I clutched the dangling steel triangle and pulled myself to an upright position. Within a split second the dagger-like pain pierced my torso like millions of needles penetrating a human pincushion. The gut-wrenching pain kept sweeping over me, one wave after another. I braced myself and firmly griped the metal handle. I was holding on for dear life. I didn't want to go back down again.

With the assistance of the steadying hand of the nurse and the numbing effect of the medication, I was able to thwart the urge to fall back. It wasn't pretty and it was awfully slow going, but it was a beginning. Forget the quick-and-one-motion notion I had concocted. This was slow and harrowing work.

A few choice words later and I was proudly sitting upright, of my own accord. But that position was short-lived. Only seconds after my gloating began I was tackled at my midriff by an overwhelming stabbing sensation. Instinct pulled me backward, down toward the comforting horizontal position. Within seconds of my victory I abandoned my perpendicular position and was forced to make a mattress crash landing.

I was distraught. Although engulfed by a deluge of physical agony, it wasn't the pain that hurt most. No, worse than the mere physical trauma was the mental anguish that tugged at my heartstrings. There I was right back where I had begun so many pains ago. I lay there staring at the ceiling, full of anger and frustration the tears welling up in the corners of my eyes. In one split second I'd lost all the ground I'd made. With my bladder still full and no stock pot in sight, there was no choice but to do it all over again.

Nurse Ratchet was still in her bedside position, spouting off words of encouragement. Just what I needed to hear! In a tortuous tone of voice she rattled on. "Don't be discouraged. This happens all the time. You can do it, come on, you have to."

At that very moment I wanted to reach across and slap her, claw her, inflict bodily harm. However, I'm not a violent person. So I was thankful the thought was just a thought, and fleeting at that. I'm sure it was temporary insanity—maybe even the drugs.

Laying there on my back, moaning and groaning, the seconds and minutes seemed to turn into hours. Tension filled the air as the nurse gave me yet another of her compassionate pep talks.

"Take your time," she smiled and said affectionately. "No need to be a hero. Easy does it."

Yeah right. Too late to claim that *hero* title, I thought to myself as I managed to suppress the desire to bark some of my own orders back at her. Tell my bladder to take its time because right here and right now I don't have the luxury of taking my time. I gotta pee like a racehorse; and thanks to you and your overeager desire to pull my pee-pee pipeline, there's nowhere to tinkle but the toilet. And between here and there is the longest distance and the hardest floor. But at least I curtailed my verbal urge.

My husband stood helplessly by my bedside, unable to will me to the bathroom. I wanted to kick her and yell at him; or vice-versa, it didn't really matter. I just wanted to vent my frustrations over not being able to pee in my own time, in my own way, of my own volition, and especially without an audience.

I needed to be alone to lick my wounds and fight this battle on my own. My head and body were already in action exchanging fighting words. Move, I command you. In the name of recovery, move your bones upward and outward! The internal war waged within me. No way, it hurts too much. Pain, pain, go away, come again another day, my saner side mocked back.

I waited patiently as my mind and body argued over when, where and how we would best solve this pee-pee problem. After a minute or two of just chilling out, a childhood choo-choo story came to mind and, with it, the familiar tune that propelled me into action. As I positioned myself for another try, I repeated over and over to myself, *I think I can. I think I can. I think I can.*

Only a few verses later I was changing my tune to *I knew I could. I knew I could.* Mind over matter and I was up and at 'em, sitting bedside, ready to take on the tile. I paused and caught my breath. I just sat—well, sort of sat. I was doubled over clutching my tummy.

Then all of a sudden it hit me. I was shocked. Just a mere 1,500 minutes after a scalpel had toured my tummy, my stomach had been stapled, my muscles turned to mush, and my womb robbed of its treasures, I was sitting up on the side of the bed with my feet dangling over the side. So much for laying back and taking it easy.

The only thing left to do was walk the walk. It began oh-so-slow. Gently, I slid one foot down to the floor. Then came the other. Deep breath, lean forward, totter up onto wobbly legs. Then one foot in front of the other. There it was, an actual step. It was like riding a bike. Eureka! I hadn't forgotten how to walk. I was actually doing the toilet tango, slowly gliding, shuffling along to my own solo song of moaning and groaning.

As I shuffled, I clutched my tummy in fear that at any moment my wound would rip open and my insides would splatter all over the linoleum. Since I am on an honest path here, I have to admit that I did not actually walk, in the truest since of the word. It was more of a duck-like waddle. The difference being that a duck waddles in an upright stance and I was doubled over in a position the Hunchback of Notre Dame would have envied.

I won't lie; the trip was not a pleasant journey. Matter of fact, I will venture to say that it was horrendous. It was both an agonizing, and frightful trek that defied the numbing effects of my pain medication. But never mind all of that, I was just relieved, for my "tinkle debut" was about to begin.

So focused on the challenge, I had almost forgotten the purpose of my mission by the time I arrived at my destination. One look down at the toilet and it all came flooding back. Unfortunately, with that downward glance came more than just the memory of my mission.

Now, what I found in my *private* bathroom, in my *private* hospital room, would make any woman go absolutely crazy, not to mention a cranky, hurting, drugged woman who had just lost her ovaries and, with them, all emotional stability (assuming she ever had any to begin with). Imagine my horror when finally, after overcoming all the odds, walking of my own volition, encountering untold pain and agony, after all the bravery I had to muster to make this journey, I arrived at my destination only to discover the unthinkable!

There it was right before my very eyes, the naked bowl stood before me. There was no lid, there was no ring, and there was no thing but a bare bowl. The seat of my throne was displaced. Let me make this perfectly clear: That very invention on which women of the world have positioned themselves on for decades, was not where it was intended to be. The ring of my private privy was in the "up" position!

Some man had committed the unbelievable act of lifting and leaving! An act that, by itself, was terrible enough, but here in the women's ward of the hospital? The one sacred place where women are the only patients and, as such, the only ones privileged to use the plumbing. In this exclusive unit men are considered true outsiders and, as such, are expected to use the *Men's Room* down the hall. It is one of the few benefits of bearing all the pain of womanhood.

I just stood there in my semiconscious, pain-pilled state of mind, dazed, and shaking as the knots in my stomach tightened, and the rage began to rise, leaving the red of anger to color my postoperative pale complexion. Only one could possibly be guilty of this offensive offense. My husband was the only man that had entered my sanctuary and stayed long enough to be in need of relief. Of all the places and all the times, how could he? What in the world was he thinking? How could he, I wondered, even think of such a dastardly deed as first trespassing, and then leaving his manly mark on the toilet intended solely for me?

This should have been the one time, the one place where I would be safe, certain not to fall victim to the fate of a rising ring, and guaranteed that my maiden voyage would not be a voyage to the bottom of the bowl.

As I stood there, staring at the commode in utter horror, I was convinced of one thing. When it comes to the territorial toilet tiff, this proved that some men are both shameless and incorrigible!

Now, I don't have many pet peeves, but the few I do have are very special to me and I'm adamant about them. Nothing can set my mouth spewing faster than experiencing one of my peeves. A Sunday driver, any day of the week, just tooling along in what is supposed to be the fast lane, gets my blood boiling and blood pressure escalating at a record breaking pace.

However, there is one thing far more irritating to me. It grates on my nerves worse than the anything else. Being a lady, and raised by a wonderful, kind, and *proper* woman, my biggest bitch involves the proper placement of the toilet seat.

I was raised in a family wherein the can was not an issue in our home. The males (brothers and father alike) were properly trained, my mother saw to it. In our household it was required that the ring always be returned to its proper position, which we had been taught was resting down on the rim. No questions, no debates, no arguments. My father knew, and my two brothers knew. It was the law of the land. Anything different was an opportunity for me to "nark" on my male counterparts, which I joyfully did every time the occasion arose.

"Mom, the toilet seat was left up," I would yell from the facility. Then, let the games begin! I would sit back, listen, and watch as mom went on her warpath. Each male in the household would be interrogated, questioned, drilled, examined, and then cross-examined until the culprit was found, guilt was admitted, and proper punishment administered.

Oh, those were the good ole days. But that was then and this was now. I was not at home with my mother, and she obviously had not trained my husband.

As previously mentioned, I was a late bloomer and, as such, did not marry until I was "mature." Then it took only a few months of *marital bliss* to figure out why I had so wisely waited. Even as newlyweds, it didn't take long for the subject of the toilet seat to come up between my mate and me. As a career bachelorette, I was not prepared for all that accompanies living with another, twenty-four hours a day, seven days a week, twelve months a year until death do us part.

The john remains a source of contention between my husband and me. Whether home or hotel, guest bathroom or master bath, family or friends' the proper placement of the ring prompts recurrent debates between us. I have yelled. I have pleaded. I have bribed. After hitting cold water in the middle of the night, I have even threatened bodily harm. All to no avail. No matter how hard I try to put a lid on this problem, it keeps popping up.

This dilemma has even extended outside our marriage, making it truly a family matter. On at least one occasion my mother has encountered the unpleasant experience of testing the waters during a nocturnal dunk in her own toilet. It was, of course, after her favorite (only) son-in-law paid her a visit.

I have bitched continuously, propositioned affectionately, and confidentially considered male finishing school. Nothing has worked. I have laid money on the line by placing a jar labeled potty toll on top of the commode and having my husband deposit a quarter every time he left the seat up. The jar filled, yet still I fumed. I upped the ante and raised the stakes to one dollar per incident. Every time he got relieved, I got a dollar richer. Neither one of us seemed willing to give in or to compromise. Yes, this ring ruckus has taken its toll on our marriage.

In desperation, earlier in our marriage, I went so far as to draft a letter to a famous advice columnist seeking assistance on this persistent problem. It went like this:

Dear Abby,

I am sure you have loads of these letters, so hopefully one more won't matter because if my dilemma doesn't get solved soon, my marriage may find itself in divorce court before our one-year anniversary. I have never been married before so I am only now, at the ripe old age of thirty-seven, discovering the good, bad, and ugly of being with a man on a daily basis. Most of which I can handle, and that which I cannot handle I am learning to endure, with only one exception. The endless trial and tribulation over the toilet. I was raised in a home where my brothers and father lowered the toilet seat after each use, and were taught that any other placement was simply rude and ill-mannered behavior, which was not tolerated under my mother's roof. My husband, on the other hand, doesn't understand this concept and seems to take real sick pleasure in pushing my button via the toilet. The problem is becoming a major source of contention in our household and one that prompts relentless wifely whimpering. For peace's sake I have offered a compromise. Instead of spreading his misery throughout our home I suggested that my husband declare any two of our three bathrooms as his own territory to do with the ring as he sees fit. I would have the remaining one so that I could squat with the security of knowing I have a seat to sit on. But no, this was not agreeable. I even suggested for fairness sake that we both be required to put the ring and lid down when we finish, but he didn't keep his end of the bargain, conveniently claiming forgetfulness. I am seeking your advice. My patience is running thin where this subject is concerned and I am at my wit's (and wife's) end. Do you think leaving the ring up is really rude, or was I just raised with an overly polite mother? The idea of building an outhouse in the backyard is becoming more appealing with every late night sojourn wherein my bottom sinks to low (and wet) levels.

Had I actually sent the letter, I would have signed me *Peeved About The Potty Problem.*

Oh, but this time he had gone too far. He had crossed the line. To make me BEND in my condition for the sole purpose of lowering the seat so I could tinkle on my first outing after undergoing surgery, was unbearable, almost unforgivable. Had I been thinking clearly, I would really have gotten him by taking an embarrassing course of action that just might have permanently convinced him of the proper position of the ring—at least in the women's ward of a hospital. This fantasy plan, I am convinced, would have broken him of his irritating, chauvinistic habit.

Without tinkling, I should have shuffled back to my bed and rang the nurses call button. Once she answered, my pleas would not only embarrass my husband but also, hopefully, shock him into submission. My words, as they were transmitted over the intercom, would have echoed through the halls of the maternity ward for all women to hear . . .

Nurse, I cannot go to the bathroom because the seat to my toilet is in the up position and I am in no condition to try to sit on the rim. Would you send someone to put it down for me? I just had a hysterectomy, and I'm not yet able to bend enough to do it myself. I have no idea who would have done such an insensitive thing as to use my toilet and then leave the seat up. No matter now, because I just made my first painful trip to the bathroom, all for naught, because I cannot sit. So would you please help me?

I could only imagine his reaction as the monologue reverberated for the entire ward to hear. His coloring would have changed from tan to a brilliant beet red. Immediately my other half would dash to the bathroom in an attempt to conceal (lower) the evidence. The clanking sound of the toilet seat being slammed down in utter embarrassment would thunder throughout the room, filtering outward, eventually sounding through the halls of the entire women's wing.

A chorus of laughter rolling down the corridor would answer.

Then he would run back to my bedside, grab the call button out of my hand just in time to catch the nurse before she journeys down the hall to answer my desperate call. I would then look up at him with a mischievous expression and a small, very small, impish grin on my face. Unable to hold back any longer, I would let go the pent-up laughter and my stitches would all pop open.

Oh, but the last laugh, it would have been well worth it! Had I been thinking clearly, my dream would have become reality and sweet revenge would have been mine. Well, I guess hindsight truly is 20-20.

I really was in no mood for jokes or lessons, much less anything that would cause me to repeat my trek to the bathroom. So reluctantly, angrily, and oh-so-painfully, I managed to *bend* over, unfortunately from the waist (the same waist which was recently and currently tied, tightened, held, and sewn together by thread, staples, and tape) enough to reach the ring, grab it, and let it go in a free-fall fashion.

Immediately gravity took control and the plastic perch fell all the way to its rightful, downward position atop the bowl. CLANKKKKK! The sound reverberated from one bathroom wall to another. Yes, I did let it drop *hard*, hoping that my husband would at least hear the horribly loud sound of the ringing rim and feel deep remorse.

Once properly positioned, I was free to struggle into a sitting position on the throne. It was an opportunity for me to stew a little longer about my husband's inconsiderate behavior. However, these ill thoughts were soon replaced with impatience over my bladder's unwillingness to cooperate in the matter at hand. Although commanding that organ to dispense with all stored within, nothing came forth. I willed it, then waited, and waited some more. The more I sat, the madder I got. Nothing was happening. I just sat there, willing, waiting, and wooing . . .

Tinkle, tinkle little stream. Come on, I know you are in there. We can do this. We have been doing this all our lives, without prompting, without problems. I know you are capable, I coaxed my stubborn pipes.

After five minutes my attitude changed. Forget the

stream. Could we manage droplets? Okay, I won't even ask for that much. At this point I'd settle for one little, tiny, tinny drop!

But zip, nada, nothing! Not one single tinklet came forth. I yelled to the nurse, patiently waiting outside the bathroom door, to please turn on the water faucet. That always does the trick. However, not this time, not this trip.

I sat there, elbow resting on my leg and chin propped on my fist, and pondered my possibilities. My choices were limited. I could sit here all day or waddle back to bed and lie in defeat until the urge hit again. Then I'd have to do this all over. Sitting and deciding, deciding and sitting. What is a patient to do? What a predicament this was. Pee or flee?

Finally, after careful contemplation and a thorough review of the options, I asked the nurse one last, subdued question.

"Can I try later?" I dejectedly inquired.

I managed to waddle back to the bed, slowly and painfully crawl back into the safety of my bed, back to the tranquility of a drug-induced stupor. Sleep, I wanted to sleep, not pee. That would come later, but for now I wanted only to dive into a deep sleep. That was my last thought as I resumed my slumber.

The memory of that moment, my maiden voyage, the bathroom debut managed to stay with me quite some time. I sat so long on the throne that a temporary toilet tattoo appeared on my rear. There on my backside was a semicircle; at least half of the toilet seat was there on my seat, a flesh impression of my precious ring.

FIVE

The Long
Gurney Home

Having made the trip, having passed the pee-pee test, there were no more obstacles between me and the comforts of my home, or so I thought.

Only a few hours after the surgery I discovered, to my horror, that a section of my abdomen below my belly button was held together, not by nylon cord, nor cotton thread, but by metal staples. I was stitched inside and out. Internally and externally, foreign matter tied my tummy together.

I was certain that these metal staples would not deteriorate with time, as would the internal absorbable suture, which lined my insides. No, I was afraid there was only one way these ugly things would leave my body—removal. This caused great concern. From the time I got out of recovery and discovered the things, worry set in. Then I learned the staples would have to come out *before* I departed the hospital. And so I worried some more. Now, with my discharge imminent, I feared this removal travail was fast approaching.

I didn't think they would forget such a small detail as to let me leave with tin embedded in my tummy. Unfortunately, I was correct in my assumption. I saw her coming and immediately knew what she was after. It must have been the fact Ms. Edward Scissorhands was wielding a tool resembling a pair of pliers, the blinding glare of a metallic instrument shining in my face as she approached my bed. There was no question about it; the moment had indeed arrived. Just what I needed in my delicate condition, a little bit more pain.

"Will it hurt?" I whined pitifully as she fixed on her target.

"No. You will feel only some slight pressure."

Yeah right. How many times has metal wire been plucked with pliers from your tender war-torn skin? I wanted to ask her. But she held the tool. So I held my tongue. Restraint was definitely in order here.

Surprisingly, the ordeal was relatively pain-free. Of course, that is from the warped perspective of a woman who just had her womb cut out. The important thing is I survived, and managed to overcome one more home-going hurdle.

However, with the removal of the metal came another problem, another thing to worry about. The shiny metal staples were replaced with twelve (yeah, I did count them) pieces of tape—the adhesive and clingy type. Those things, too, would have to be removed in time, two weeks to be exact. I began fretting yet again. I had a couple weeks to contemplate how they would remove those little strips that, in a fourteen-day period, would surely graft to my skin.

However there were more pressing issues at hand. Today, there was a form of relief within sight. I was going to be sprung from this sterile environment. Home! I was going to the restful pleasures of my own home where I could lick my wounds in peace, wallow in self-pity privately. Homeward bound I was, and none too soon.

I only thought my trip to the bathroom was rough. It was a piece of cake compared to the 40-mile cross-country expedition home. The entire experience, from start to finish, was nothing short of tortuous. It began with getting out of bed, getting dressed, and then graduated to posturing a position in a wobbly wheelchair.

Whether wheeled chairs or steel-belted radials, rubber definitely is not a shock *absorber*. From hallways to highways, my stitched stomach detected each and every single, solitary lump and bump along the entire stretch home. With each jiggle of my gut came a moan from my mouth. It was such a wonderful time for both my chauffeur/husband and me. Given a choice in the matter he would have been the last person on my list of desirable drivers.

There are very few things in life that really frighten me, and my spouse's maneuvering of a motor vehicle is one. On the hairy-scary scale it ranks right up there, only one notch below skydiving without a reserve parachute. I am constantly amazed he is actually accident free, which can only be attributed to other drivers being very attentive. He is the type that looks for wildlife while driving. Even more amazing, he spots the camouflaged animals on the horizon long before I do.

On road trips I find comfort in burying my nose in a newspaper, figuring that what I cannot see will not hurt me. It works until I discover that my husband, while driving, is not only reading across the front seat, but finishes the same article long before me!

It's no wonder then I dreaded the drive home. Once in the vehicle's passenger seat, the paranoia set in. Now, my husband is not only a carefree, careless, and fast driver, but he also has no comprehension of the pain involved with womanhood. He didn't understand all the fuss about a few cramps, so I was more than a little concerned about how he would handle this incision situation. With a pillow pressed against my stomach for support, I literally braced for the worse. From the copilot's seat I started barking orders before the poor man even got into the driver's seat.

"Easy with my seat! Don't slam the car door," I yelled as he attempted to assist me into the cockpit.

And the orders did not cease once we were on our way. I was wide awake, bound and determined to help him drive, for my health reasons. I appointed myself to the lookout post. From the hospital parking lot, along the state highway, to our driveway, I constantly watched for bumps, big and small, pointing them out and then pleading for mercy.

"Be careful. Go slow. Watch that speed bump. Oh pleeeeasssse go around it! There's a big hole in the road. Would you please miss it, too? Oooooooch!"

My pleas progressed as the trip lengthened—and the speed increased. Quickly the white stripes on the highway turned to a single, solid white line; telephone poles brown blurs. Traveling at the speed of a Concord jet it was hard for me to see many of the potholes before we flew into and out of them. We hit so many I began to wonder if he was warning me of the damage he could inflict if I didn't quiet down and leave the driving to him. However, I knew my sweet, wonderful man would never think such evil thoughts or engage in such dastardly deeds. How it happened I'll never know, but to my complete surprise, we arrived home safely, with my tummy intact.

Bearing the Big H

Oh the miracles of thread and tape!

Once home, my husband wasted no time in getting me into bed and administering sleep-inducing drugs. He never said anything, but I detected he was in need of some quiet time. And this was just the first hour of my six-week recovery period.

In the beginning, the first few days after surgery, I felt great—as if I could do anything. A friend who had also undergone the Big H told me she felt so great the day after her surgery that she hit the floor running, or at least walking. I must admit that I didn't really believe her then. However, after experiencing the same postoperative rush, I knew she had not been exaggerating.

Although two days after surgery I felt good and well enough to go home and fend for myself, the *Super Woman* mode did not last. I was unable to completely appreciate and comprehend the doctor's orders of complete pelvic rest until I personally experienced the teeth-gritting, suture-straining, pain-provoking act of closing a window.

My first night home was a welcome relief from the hospital and the steady stream of intruding medical personnel. I looked forward to a restful, private, and peaceful night in my own bed. However, despite the morphine pain pills I swallowed only hours earlier, I found myself battling a bad case of insomnia. It must have been all the lingering excitement from the drive home.

It was one o'clock in the morning when I decided to crawl out of bed, literally. Call it lack of brains or being under the influence, but whatever the reason, I found myself *climbing* upstairs to my computer. Now, that was a real trip. I was medicated enough that the physical action of raising each foot, step by step, did not hurt. However, sitting in an upright position on a stiff hard chair in front of my computer was an entirely different story. After only five minutes, I found myself clutching my stomach and retreating down the stairs to the softness of the sofa.

Then it began. First came the echo of thunder breaking the silence of the night, followed by lightening illuminating the room as it pierced through the black veil of darkness. Then gentle sounds of raindrops landing on the leaves outside the big plate glass window began. Pink, dink, dink, pink. The little droplets fell so softly.

There is nothing more serene to me than the sound of Mother Nature watering her treasures. The gift of a spring shower was being delivered outdoors. The sounds were relaxing, and I nestled onto the sofa and drifted off to sleep as the lullaby played outside the patio door.

Plank, plank, plunk, thud, thunk! Suddenly I awoke as the soft sounds of Mother Nature's orchestra were replaced by the dissonant cacophony of heavy metal music. The pounding of raindrops on the roof rustled me to attention. The spring shower had changed into a full-blown thunderstorm, complete with a drenching downpour.

Quickly I rose from my makeshift bed and walked over to the window—the open window! An unsolicited, unassisted carpet cleaning was underway, compliments of the torrential, blowing rain. Therefore, I did what any normal person would do under these stormy circumstances. I reached up and, with all my might, forcefully pushed and then pulled the glass frame downward. It was an automatic reaction. I did it without thinking. And I did it with all my strength.

However, there was a small problem. I forgot I was *not* normal. It was only as I squatted and pulled hard that I remembered where I had been, what had occurred only a few days earlier. Okay, so I didn't really remember, more like rudely reminded, in a unkind manner, that my belly was full of stitches and my muscles were only mush.

As the pain progressed downward, I immediately doubled over and grabbed my stomach. Once I was convinced that my remaining organs would not be spilling onto the carpet below me, I very carefully and slowly found my way back to the safety of my bed. There I remained for the rest of the night and into the next day. I feared the worst, a busted stitch and/or destruction of my doctor's four-inch masterpiece.

Once so simple, the task of closing a window became a great source of strain—and pain. Oh the pain! Oh the strain! Oh the stupidity! I never imagined, never thought that the doctor's order of pelvic rest included the prohibition of closing a window, saving a sill. After all, the song does not say that the pelvic bone is connected to the stomach muscles. (After months of recovery, I guarantee that the stomach muscles are connected to every part of the body in one way or the other). Although it had been over twenty years since I had taken a human anatomy course, this operation served a huge reminder of how much midsection muscles are used in the course of everyday living.

My doctor failed to mention the condition (or lack of condition) of my muscles. He didn't tell me they were crippled, and he failed to warn me not to do *anything* for a week or so. No, I had to learn this the same way I had learned so much in my life—the hard way. I never thought that walking, bending, sitting, and just plain moving, in any manner, in any direction, would get my attention in such a negative way.

Very early the next morning I called the doctor, asking him the question that loomed overhead since my airhead move. I was afraid the gut-wrenching, window-closing attempt had done some major damage to his handy work.

"Hey Doctor, do you think pulling a stitch is possible with such a ploy?" I inquired after describing my (lack of) behavior.

His reply was, as always, full of humor. What did I expect from my young(er) wanna-be-comedian doctor.

"I know you; and therefore I used extra heavy-duty string for the stitches, the type which would snag a 50-pound flathead catfish," (and keep a 100-plus pound dumb head together after surgery. I'm sure he was also thinking at that moment).

However the good doctor didn't seem too alarmed at my stupidity. The prescribed therapy for the strain was bed rest (duh) and a heating pad.

Despite what my husband may say, I can follow doctor's orders, and with this latest escapade, I was now ready, more than ever, to do so. So, without hesitation, I journeyed to the bathroom, found the heating pad and made the trip to my sofa. Who would have thought that a simple doctor's order of using a heating pad would cause yet another crisis in my recovery?

With heating pad in hand, I was set to hit the sofa and get horizontal for the day, just me, my pad, and my pain. As I readied myself and my accompanying electrical appliance, a minor problem surfaced. There were only two electrical plugs in the entire living room, one strategically located *way behind* the stereo and the other *way behind* the sofa—like exactly in the middle of the lengthy, heavy couch. Having just realized my own physical limitations bending, stretching, pushing or crawling for an electrical source was not an option. Obviously, moving furniture was completely beyond my current abilities, and completely out of the question.

Now, some may say I am dumb, but I certainly am not stupid. I realized there was little I could do to get the juice flowing to my pad. So I did what any rational, hormone-deprived woman would do in this situation. I sat down and cried. Although it may not have accomplished much, it felt good. Once the overflow of tears ended, I called my mother and explained my situation. Living six miles away, she was willing only to suggest I call my husband for help.

"Mom, don't you think he was my first choice? However, he does work for a living, and he just happens to be in a meeting now. Never mind, I don't want to interrupt one of your coveted retirement moments," I quipped sarcastically. So much for motherly love.

I was about to indulge myself again in another of my own pity parties when the sound of a possible rescue caught my ears. The metal monotone of a truck door slamming outdoors gave me hope. My neighbor was home, outside, and within reach! With a pillow pressed to my tummy, I waddled outside and pitifully beckoned for help.

Now, my neighbor is not what I would classify as overly neighborly. He would probably never be crowned *Mr. Personality*. Notwithstanding, he could be relied upon for aid. For many, many years, he'd been trained, and paid, to do just that in the police department.

We have never had more than a fence friendship. I speak to him through the wooden fence (my height dictates that it is only through and not over), and he responds accordingly back over the fence. Sometimes I wish we were on friendlier grounds. He and his wife are, after all, the neighbors that know all our comings and goings due to the strategic location of their kitchen window. However, I don't think he likes my dog and this has causes some tension that won't be resolved until one of them passes on.

But this all seems to go by the wayside whenever I need his help. Last summer he really proved that when our backyard resembled Medusa's head. Snakes, the size of boa constrictors, were literally coming out of the woodwork. Under the fence, and even through a hole in the wooden fortress they slithered into the yard. I had never seen anything like it!

I don't mind snakes. I used to play with them when I was a kid, capturing them and keeping them prisoner, writhing in the confines of a glass jar. I'd treat the slithery reptile like a normal pet, naming it and feeding it. The best part was showing it off to my friends and scaring the pants off the girly types. They would squeal and run away at the sight of my coiled companion and its darting forked tongue. But that was then and this was now. I am older, wiser, more careful, much more cautious and a whole lot pickier about my playmates.

One snake I could take, but two that were "eating" size was too much. Adding to the disdain was not knowing their type, their breed, whether poisonous or playful. And I do have two dogs that venture outside whenever the mood strikes. So I called my neighbor and explained the situation to his wife. Within minutes my shovel-wielding warrior was on the scene. You could tell by his walk that he was on a mission and ready for the challenge. He is a retired police officer, accustom to helping people in a crisis.

Being an animal lover, I didn't want him to kill the snakes, only tell me if they were poisonous. I watched from the patio as he took command. Like a true detective, he cautiously eased forward along the fence for a closer look, careful not to get too close, too quickly.

Then without warning there was a deafening WHAM! WHAM! I couldn't look; sadness filled me at the thought of a living creature's life being needlessly cut (in half). However, I couldn't let my guardian detect my unhappiness over his shovel-happy heroics. I thanked him and he left, fortunately unable to find the other snake.

A few hours later, while waiting for my husband to come home and properly dispose of the snake, I noticed the dead creature had moved, and quite a distance for the dead to move! I watched from the inside, waiting to see what was causing the lifeless to linger, the dead to come alive. Then I saw it. Another snake was there pulling the lifeless one under the fence. As I watched from the window my emotions went into overdrive, as did my imagination.

My heart bled as the pitiful play, the sickening scene unfolded before my eyes. It was the wife coming to take the dear, departed husband home to her orphaned children for a proper burial. Without a husband's support and a father's guidance the surviving family members were suspectible to a problem-plagued existence.

A year had passed since I had called on the assistance of my assassin neighbor. Not too soon to ask again, I thought. Just the sight of my sickly shuffle across the yard should have convinced him I was indeed in need of help. Surely, he wouldn't have to draw on his years of detective experience to realize I was in dire straits.

The sight of this downtrodden woman with red, puffy eyes, clad in her nightgown at noon did not even faze the good man. Without posing a question or raising an eyebrow, he followed me inside the house as I detailed my latest dilemma. He went straight to the source of the problem, bent over and plugged in my pad. A sigh of relief from me signaled my appreciation. I couldn't thank him enough, and the more I gushed on, the more embarrassed he seemed to become. Quickly he headed for the front door with a few simple pleasant parting words.

"If you need anything else, just call me, anytime, and I'll come on over and help ya."

I didn't see hide or hair of him after that. Of course, I wasn't out cruising around the yard looking for him either. Nevertheless, after seeing me, and assisting me, I am willing to bet he barricaded the door, immediately installed Caller ID on his telephones and then turned up the tunes to drown out any ringing doorbells or the pleas from the next-door ding-a-ling.

SIX

Never a
Dull Movement

I had been informed. I had been forewarned. Yet nothing prepared me for the lengthy roller coaster ride of recovery. My recuperation in the first weeks went something like this: pain pill, gas, stool softener, pain pill, hormonal hemorrhage (emotional outburst), gas, tears, more tears, bitch, bitch, bitch (dramatic complaining), pain pill, nap (i.e. brief peace for everyone). During this tumultuous period, I was inclined to frequently remind my husband, in a sarcastic tone of voice, of a promise he had made only a few short years earlier.

"Darling, Dear Heart, remember you *vowed* (with an emphasis on that one word) to love me in sickness and in bad times." It was intentional that I always omitted referring to the "in health and in good times" verbiage. That part was not pertinent to my point.

I am not a "pitiful" person. Never have I purposely conducted myself in a manner that would lead anyone to think otherwise. Never has anything in my life caused people to feel sorry for me. No, I pride myself on being a pity-free person.

Along with this characteristic I'd cultivated self-sufficiency. I am an independent person, fully capable of taking care of myself always have been. After eighteen years of being single and on my own, I took for granted doing things my way. I didn't want or need anyone to take care of me. I had spent my life perfecting the art of independence.

That was before the Big H. Let me tell you, a hysterectomy removes more than female organs. It totally robs a woman of her independence, at least temporarily. I had never fully comprehended or appreciated my autonomy until a four-inch incision across the grain of my stomach muscles rendered me helpless (and useless, but I couldn't admit to that).

Now I was in a distressing situation, having to speak a

foreign language. Words and phrases I was not accustomed to were actually coming from my own mouth. Things like: *Would you please help me? I can't do it. I need . . .*

So many times during the day, and night, those pathetic pleas came forth from my lips. It didn't take long for me to grow very weary of saying formerly forbidden things such as *I can't* and *please help me.* Those whimpers were followed by the barrage of begging of anyone within earshot, with pleading phrases, such as: Would you . . .? and Could you . . .?

Pages could be written and I could go on for hours about the things this surgery causes a person to have to request from others. However, all appeals center around one thing—a four-letter word; namely help.

Life as I had known it changed. Now, in addition to all the emotional, physical and mental adjustments I was having to deal with, I was confronted with helplessness for the first time in my life. It was a major source of difficulty. Obviously, some reprogramming was necessary. My situation, and limitations, made that happen quickly.

For the first few days I was as dependent and helpless as a newborn kitten. I certainly couldn't fend for myself. Family members, those brave enough to volunteer for duty, were always within shouting distance. And, except when slumber set in, there was always some sort of beckoning or bellowing going on. As hard as it is for me to admit, I had to have help with everything.

Every small facet of my life seemed to require assistance. I needed help getting into and out of bed—and while there, I needed help rolling over. I needed help walking to and from the sofa for a change of scenery. I needed help getting water so I could take my medication. I also needed help getting dressed as well as help getting to, getting on, and getting off the potty. Help, help, help, help, help! That word was uttered and muttered so often it became another dirty four-letter word to me—and those poor souls around me.

I will never know whether he had tired or if it was actually time, but after two days of being my full-time nurse, my husband went back to work, leaving me to fend for myself. So no one was around if I needed assistance. I faced this reality squarely when I needed help reaching the toilet paper. (Oh yes, there is yet one more toilet tale to be told). Being stranded is bad enough on a good day, but it's even worse during recovery. I accepted the fact my spouse had to go back to work and thought I could probably manage all alone. I was not prepared however for the bachelor condition of our home. I had been absent for only two days and in bed another few days, so I wondered how the house could become so discombobulated in such a short period of time. Nothing was as I had left it. Nothing was as it should have been. And true to my life story, I discovered this the hard way, quite by accident.

Within only hours of my husband's departure there was a calling that caused me to get up, and out of bed. Unfortunately, this was a feat that was both dreaded and painful. Carefully, oh-so-carefully I managed to move. In the last few days, I had acquired an appendage. Used as stomach support, my pillow became a part of my tummy. Without much fanfare I managed to make the short trek to the toilet in the master bathroom. I also managed the more difficult feat of *bending* to sit down.

As soon as the flow began, I noticed a peculiar sight before me. The toilet paper roll was at its end, causing me to be at my wit's end! Desperately I eyed the empty roll on the holder, the cylinder shell of brown cardboard staring back. This is another bachelor boo-boo. Only there were no bachelors in our home, only lingering bachelor bad habits.

Anxiety overcame me as I contemplated the whereabouts of a refill roll. I fumed at the lack of paper and the continual lack of my husband's toilet etiquette. I was home alone with no one to rescue me, no one to hear my pitiful pleas.

As a child I never really cared for the game of hide and seek. It never thrilled me like other childhood games. But being stranded on the bowl without a replacement roll within eyesight or arm's length (as it always had been and always should be) I was forced to play the game. It may be entertaining when the searching is only for fun, but I consider it cruelty when the object of the search is a necessity. And this particular paper product is always classified as a feminine necessity.

I climbed off my throne, making certain all the drips

had dropped, and began searching high and low for that elusive roll. I knew where it was *supposed* to be. And had I been in charge of the household, at least a four-pack would have been there. So first I rummaged through the obvious, usual; and nearby locations. A roll was nowhere to be found inside the cabinets under the bathroom sink. From there my hunt took me into the guest bathroom across the hall, but again no sight of any paper products fit for the chore.

So early in my recovery, the stairway was still off-limits by doctor's orders. Therefore, a gander into the cabinets in the upstairs bathrooms was not possible. I was running out of hiding places. My worry lines deepened as my desperation increased. Not a single, solitary square of the so-squeezably-soft could be found.

I waddled back to the master bathroom to sulk when, lo-and-behold, there was a sighting! There it was, that four-pack of paper located in the most unlikely location for a woman barely five feet two inches tall. Way up, on *top* of the cabinet some seven feet high, way out of my short reach, was the object of my desire.

Normally this would not have been a big deal. I would have climbed up on the toilet lid and reached for the roll. But that wasn't possible now that I was full of stitches that didn't take kindly to stretching. I thought about attempting the feat but decided not to test fate. Frustrated, I decided to just sit back down on the bowl and drip dry. While drying, I passed the time cussing the rocket scientist that put it up there!

This was only the beginning of the long, winding road to recovery. It seemed that there was always one dilemma after another. My first few days were spent adjusting to my limited mobility and learning to cope with not being physically able to do things for myself. It was strain as well as a drain—for us all. I was tired of the situation. I wanted some sort of independence if only for a fleeting moment. Desperate and determined, I hit on something. However small, it was a start.

After almost a week of waddling around barefooted on my dirt-laden tile floors, I realized the importance of a pair of slippers. Not just any type of slippers, but real "slip"pers, which do not require bending at the waist to get the elastic over the heel. The easy walk-in kind was in order.

From flannel gray to flashy gold, to booties of red, pink, and floral, and ballerinas of black, I had every imaginable color and style of house shoes—a closet full of them. However, there was one style I lacked, a very important style to a woman in my condition. I wanted, no, I needed a pair of simple slippers. Since my surgery, every time I wanted to outfit my feet with shoes I had to seek assistance.

"Honey, I need you. I need help," I would call to my other half and my Prince Charming always came to my rescue.

Upon entering the bedroom he would somehow know it was time for him to place the slippers on his Cinderella's feet. There I would be lying on the bed, with both feet sticking straight up in the air. Instinctively he would come over and gently put the house shoes on my feet. And they say fairy tales never come true.

After a time my delight in this ritual wore thin. The true slip-on type slippers now were necessary, and at this point it did not matter if they were glass, ruby, rubber, or terry cloth. So I called my husband at his office and told him how good I'd been—that I hadn't lifted or done anything off limits. Of course he always assumes when I start a conversation with a description of my good behavior that a request is imminent. And he is usually correct.

"My Darling, Dear, Sweet, Husband, do you have any plans after work?" I asked him sweetly.

"What do you want now?"

He had seen through the sweet tone of voice and the sugarcoated term of endearment. Seizing the moment as the perfect opportunity to plead my case, I smoothly continued my petition.

"Sweetie, I have been trying hard to follow doctor's order and protect my protruding tummy. It has been hard for me to have to ask for help with each and every little move and turn I take. So I thought of something that would make life a tad bit easier for us both."

"What do you want, and how much will it cost?" he replied.

"Would you mind terribly going by the department store on your way home from work and picking out a pair of slippers for me?"

"You have a closet full of slippers. Why do you

want more?"

"No, Dear. I don't have any slippers; I only have house shoes. Let me explain the difference between house shoes and slippers and how one of them requires your time and attention, while the others do not."

As I explained the situation, I knew what he was thinking. A few bucks spent means one less task to perform. They would be worth their weight in gold at almost any price.

Eagerly he agreed. So efficient in his chore, he brought not one, but two different colors and styles for me to choose from. He presented them to me with both a smug expression and a sigh of relief. It takes so little to make us happy; and the longer recovery last, the less it takes.

This was certainly true the fifth day of recuperation, when what I desired most in the world was the evasive novelty of a bowel movement. Don't laugh; this is certainly not a laughing matter. When I looked down at what was once my flat stomach, I saw what resembled not one, but two folds of fat staring back at me. Since pregnancy was now out of the question, it could only be one of two things causing this bulge below my belly button. It was either swelling or the fact I recently graduated to a diet of solid foods and with no recent release. It was, shall we say, staying with me. You get the picture. It happens every time I take pain pills. Add all the drugs, the anesthesia and such, not to mention the trauma, no wonder my system was out of sync.

I resorted to previously unthinkable techniques; the first was using a laxative, which they claim also acts as a stool softener. Stool softness? Who are they kidding anyway? If they call that soft, I shudder and cringe at the thought of being on the other end of my *movement* of joy without such an aid. Even worse was doing something I thought was reserved only for the male species, spending leisure time in the library, better known to women as the bathroom. I never understood why or how men could so easily retreat to the confines of a small room, reserved for only one thing and find a way to make it into something that it is not.

Alongside the necessities in our bathroom are books and magazines, from novels to National Geographic and

Victoria's Secret catalogs (let's not even go there). The cabinets are void of the normal paraphernalia such as tissue boxes and, instead, are littered with literature—and I use that term loosely. I never know whether to decorate the room as a bathroom or a study.

For me the bathroom doubling as a library is a man's thing. Not now. I had all I could take. Something had to go. Enough was certainly enough, and my ballooning stomach was visible proof something was about to pop. I was afraid if I poked my stomach I would sail into the air in an erratic orbit like a punctured helium balloon.

Home alone (except for the companionship of my canine kids) I would not have to sneak around and hide as I resorted to the unthinkable. For the first time in my life I was heading for the "library." As I walked down the hall, I glanced back at my dog lying on the floor. I needed reassurance that I was doing the right thing. As if she read my mind, Angel looked up at me with her big, brown eyes and gave me an approving look, which guaranteed she would never utter a bark about this moment.

"Hopefully, I'll be back soon," I assured her closing the door behind me.

There I was, seated on the only stool in the library. Reluctantly I studied my husband's literary collection. Desperate times call for desperate measures! I would prevail if it took all morning, all afternoon, and a rack full of reading material. I vowed this dilemma would vanish this day. Strangely though the daily newspaper was not among the selection before me. Why? I wondered. Oh yeah. It was in the kitchen, at the other end of the house.

Since surgery, my husband had tried hard to appease me; and it was a real chore, believe me! Every day before he left for work he would go outside, pick up the newspaper and deliver it to the kitchen cabinet so I could read it during the day. Not only that, he spoiled me further by removing the rubber bands and opening it to the front page before placing it on the counter.

This was such a special treat for me. First of all, I love to be spoiled, spoiled beyond rotten. Secondly, before surgery the placement of the daily newspaper had been a constant source of conflict between my husband and me. Back then, the paper went immediately to the periodical section of the library (a.k.a. the bathroom) where, after it was read, it would lay on the floor and accumulate day to day. Finally, the library staff, rather janitorial staff, rather maid, (also affectionately known as me the wife) would get fed up, gather the piles of print, and properly dispose of them in the recycling container. Because of his post operative pampering, the newspaper was not in the privy place as normal. So there would be no catching up on world events on this trip.

While on the pot I peered at the periodical selection before me. To my utter surprise, for some reason I selected the Victoria's Secret catalog from the library's shelf (which also doubled as the bathroom cabinet).

I thumbed through those catalogs before without any thought of the models or their shapely, voluptuous and oh-so perfect 36-24-36 figures, but now their forms captured my critical eye amassing tacky thoughts and ill feelings. Those skinny women with their buxom golden, half-naked, hard bodies were not what I needed to subject myself to at this time! I was, after all, hormonally imbalanced and unsure what form my negative reaction might take. Therefore, I decided National Geographic was more in order, and so the catalog was put in its proper place (the wastepaper basket) and I began reading an intellectual, educational story about van Gogh.

Sitting in this position in this place, I could easily relate to his insanity. The little I knew about van Gogh could be summed up in two words: artist and ear. However, after reading a very lengthy article about his life, I became very informed about the man, his life, and his art. But education was not my goal in this endeavor. At this point, my mission seemed impossible. I was still bloated, still miserable and, even worse, I was now a failure at the one constant thing in my life—my bowel movements.

I came out of the bathroom (oops, library) with magazine in hand. The dog didn't bother looking up. I started pacing the room, and out of dire desperation I began praying.

"I want a B.M. Please, dear God, would you just give me one bowel movement, soon? And after four days, could you make it one that really matters, if you know what I mean."

I've always been told that God hears all prayers but I wasn't quite certain He wanted to hear about my bodily functions, or lack there of. But it surely couldn't hurt.

While waiting for an answer to my prayer, I laid down on the sofa to watch television. Scanning the channels, I found a rerun of one of my favorite sitcoms. The only thing worse than surgically induced constipation is finally finding the urge to go at an inopportune time. And the urge interrupted the climax of the television show.

Although a rerun, it was one I hadn't seen. It was an episode in which Dorothy was to wed Lucas. On the way to the wedding she discovers the limo driver is her ex-husband who kidnaps her. Just as the big ending was about to unfold, I had to go. After waiting all this time, this was one calling I was not going to miss! So I turned the television volume way up and waddled down the hall. Listening to the ending from the library is not the same as seeing the events unfold on the screen. But reruns usually run over and over again. Besides I can't complain since my unusual, and embarrassing prayer was answered. And with the end of my constipation came the end of the anticipation—as well as the end of this taboo topic.

SEVEN

Taking Stock

During recuperation I was well behaved most of the time, especially at first. I went in to this recovery process wholeheartedly committed to carefully following doctor's orders to the tee most of the time. But for days upon days, hour after hour, for weeks at a time, I was alone and confined to the house, and only a few rooms of it. It was bound to happen sooner or later. And so it did. Boredom began to set in. Then loneliness climbed aboard, followed by temptation. Before I knew it, I was being bad.

There is no excuse for my behavior other than the lengthy healing process. The longer it drug on, the more adventurous I became. In no time at all, I began to break the rules, a few at a time. My first offense was the window catastrophe. Then I graduated to doing more daring and intentional things like sneaking upstairs to my beloved, noncritical new computer.

Climbing stairs was still a no-no, but the Internet called out to me. Hindsight being what it is, I must admit this was not a smart move. For reasons I shall explain, it set me back a little physically, mentally, and emotionally. A big part of it was the physical exertion involved in raising and lowering both legs and feet on each and every stair some thirty times round trip. But other extraneous circumstances existed.

It never seemed to fail that as soon as I made the long climb up the stairs and securely fastened my fanny, strategically positioned in front of the monitor and ready for a technical take-off I would hear a familiar sound chiming from downstairs.

Ding-dong, ding-dong. The doorbell would beckon me back down the stairs. For weeks on end no one ventured to my rehabilitation site, but once I climbed those stairs, people came to my house in droves, like women to a 50% off clearance sale.

Bearing the Big H

The first time it was a repairman. Then there was the mailman. One day a friend dropped by bearing gifts; namely, food—and the solid type at that.

Able to move only at a snail's pace, there was nothing I could do but answer the chime by bellowing back.

"Just a minute, I'm coming," my screams would descend down the stairs ahead of me.

That minute, I am sure, seemed more like 30 minutes to the poor soul patiently waiting outside in the 100-degree heat. And I know for certain that minute was more like a lifetime to me as I attempted to waddle downward in a timely fashion, without tumbling down the stairs and landing face-first before the caller waiting on the other side of the glass door.

The trip upstairs always zapped my energy, and coming down was doubly hard. So on those occasions when an intruder invaded my indulgence, I was forced to cease my insanity and remain on the lower level of the house until I could muster enough strength for another sneak attack on the stairs.

Truth be known, it was the stock market that kept me climbing for more. Our retirement portfolio was accessible via the information superhighway. I was hooked and addicted to the particular web site that would track our nest egg on a daily basis. Before surgery, I made a habit of keeping a close, watchful eye on our stocks. Since becoming somewhat computer literate, I could get a daily dose of the ups and downs of the stock market, in the comfort of my own home, thanks to my computer and the advances of modern technology. Strangely enough, my moods seemed to correlate to the movement of the stock market and the performance of our portfolio.

Although I have a business degree, with a double major in economics and business administration, knowledge is like many other things in life—if you don't use it, you lose it. In my intellectual heyday I could calculate international exchange rates at the drop of a hat, determine the beta quotient of a stock in my sleep. And I read the Wall Street Journal religiously. But there is hardly anything financial about me these days. During my college days, economics centered on textbook theories involving the laws of supply and demand. Now I have developed my own economic theories, which revolve around the laws of sales and savings.

This is a female philosophy that men just don't seem to comprehend. Will they ever come to understand that it is not how much is spent but how much is saved that matters the most? And if it's a real whopper of a bargain, then it's irrelevant whether the item is truly *needed.*

At our house the conversation is always the same when I come home with an armful of treasures purchased on sale.

"Honey, come look what I bought today" I say with the enthusiasm of a child on Christmas morning as I eagerly drag my mate toward the bags piled on the bed.

"What is all that and, more importantly, do we really need any of it?" he grumbles before he even sees the first item.

However, my enthusiasm doesn't wane as I pull my prizes from the shopping bags with the pride of a magician producing a rabbit from a hat.

"Guess how much!" I try to entice him into the spirit of the things.

"I don't know. You tell me," he sighs.

Then I quickly dismiss the irrelevant price information because the best is yet to come.

"But guess how much it originally cost? Do you know how much money I saved?" With a gleam in my eyes and wide smile on my face, I continue to boast of the highlight of my day.

"Just look at how much I saved. I can't believe it. Can you?"

He never seems to fully appreciate all the savings. I have tried for years to teach my husband this savings over cost line of reasoning. But for some unknown reason he is just incapable of fully comprehending—and fully appreciating—the underlying "womanomics" principle of saving matters most, need and cost don't rate.

Needless to say, my husband and I have never seen eye to eye on money matters. I think he sometimes questions how I ever managed a business degree. Monetarily, we're on opposite pages of the spread sheet. He believes in saving and paying cash. I like to buy while the buying is good. I say loans are for the living and saving is something done while waiting to die. My husband won't consider anything that has an interest payment attached. He firmly believes in budgeting as a way of life, the only way to live. I prefer to charge ahead and figure it out later.

Of course, I attribute our financial differences to the fact that he is more cautious and I am more venturesome. With such differing views on money matters, it is no wonder we are always trying to convince one another that "my way" is the right way. It has now turned into a contest of sorts.

I don't know why, but at time it seems my husband and I are more competitors than companions. Many things we do somehow become a source of competition. Often this can be a good thing, if you get my drift. But it can also be bad, as I am about to explain. This story has less to do with money than just the principle of the thing.

My husband is a civil engineer. He oversees our retirement funds. I considered this only fair, seeing as how he got the bulk of that money before he got me. However, that is irrelevant thanks to the community property law. Portions of *our* funds are contained in an IRA, which may be used to purchase stocks. My husband, being the nice and nervy man that he is, allows me the privilege of assisting in the stock selections.

While attending a meeting several months ago I got a tip on a pending stock split. Immediately I excused myself and using my convenient cellular telephone called my husband. After passing along the information he said he'd do some research and call our stock broker if warranted.

This was my first stock tip. The resulting investment should have been real cause for glory and gloating, because the stock did, indeed, split after rising $14. But with my hubby at the helm, the glory turned to gloom when he later made a confession as I began calculating our profits. Seems like he didn't buy the stock when I asked him to, but instead waited a week before plunging in. That was seven whole days after the stock was at a low point and also the same time the stock price rose sharply. Well, he did buy that stock and we did receive two for one in the split, but the profits—well, lets just say I didn't need a calculator to do the math.

I know I should look at the positive side, but I could only focus on what could and should have been. However, I managed to refrain from the "I told you so" stage. Instead, his punishment was seven days of emotionally power-packed, cutting and crippling verbal venom for which there is no antidote.

The only good thing that came of that whole fiasco was that I had proven myself a financial foe to be reckoned with. Now, at least, he will listen more intently to me and my woman's intuition.

In an attempt to smooth things over, acquire forgiveness, and attain a ceasefire to my cutting remarks, my husband offered to put me on his trading account. That meant I could trade without his approval. Additionally he gave me the privilege and honor of picking the next two stocks—by myself, without his overly conservative critique. I wasn't sure if the venom had dulled his senses or if he had just been reduced to the state of a desperate man.

I am not much of a gambler, at least where money is concerned. And in my opinion playing the stock market is more of a gamble than an investment. This is especially true when I am in control and it involves funding our future, our retirement. The pressure was on. I was overly cautious in picking my stocks, even doing a little research before narrowing down my selection.

Finally I selected two penny stocks, or small cap stocks, whichever is the correct lingo. Fortunately, I was able to gloat when I checked their progress—and believe me, I checked every day because we (me and my stocks) were on a steady climb upward. We were accumulating a nice profit, and I was soaring high on my overinflated ego as their prices continued to rise.

I definitely had the fever. One of the last things I did before going in for surgery was to check on my (oops, I mean our) stocks. Although my nerves were shot over the impending operation, my ego was enlarging as I discovered the prices had actually doubled since I gave the buy order to our broker only weeks earlier. Oh, am I good or what?

But once out from underneath the knife and home again, I was confined to the lower level of our abode, therefore unable to make the trip upstairs to the computer to track my prized picks. They were now moving without my close supervision, in a direction unknown to me. As I lay downstairs ignorant of the ebbs and flows of the bull market, uneasiness set in. I waited and worried. I held out as long as I could. Finally curiosity got the best of me. Unable to stand it one more moment, my weakness prevailed and my sanity failed. And I am here to say, curiosity not only kills the cat, but also can cause a real regression in recovery.

Against doctor's orders, and my better judgment, I faltered. Up the stairs I wandered and wobbled. I found my seat just as I had left it. Carefully I sat down in front of my monitor. Finally I let my fingers waltz across the keyboard, never missing a step in their familiar dance.

Once the portfolio page appeared, I was tickled pink. Of all our stocks, only my babies were in the black, tracking positive gains. The others, those that my more *experienced* husband had purchased, were in the red, on a real losing streak. To make matters even better, mine had not only gained, but also quadrupled in price during my absence.

The phrase no pain, no gain certainly applied to my outlaw sneaky peek, for the thrill I gained from the painful trip upstairs was well worth it. Admittedly, I was awfully proud of this sharp little blonde, stock-picking momma. Now both the stock prices and my ego were overinflated.

I slithered back downstairs, resumed my position on the sofa, and waited for my husband to come home from work. Afraid of being reprimanded for my total disregard of medical orders, I decided to sit on the information. However, I couldn't contain myself for long. After a week I was unable to keep a lid on my good news; my cup runneth over with excitement. Dismissing the risk of being scolded for my blatant disregard of doctor's orders, I decided to share our good fortune with my husband.

With only a slight smirk on my face, I blurted out the news of my success, bragging rights in full force! However, it had been a week since I last chanced the stairs and saw the screen. I was so certain that the stock prices would continue their upward climb; I felt it was not necessary to keep messing with my mending. Therefore, I was totally unprepared for the ensuing conversation.

"Yeah, I know your stocks had more than tripled," my

husband replied to my bragging. "Our stockbroker called late last week and told me they were really up and were beginning to fall. He asked if we wanted to sell."

"And you said...?"

"I told him no. He just wanted to make a commission on our profits," he shrugged it all off.

That would have all been fine and dandy had he kept a watchful eye on the stocks after that point. After all, the stockbroker had warned him the stock prices were falling. But no, not my husband, not with *my* stock picks. He just carried on with life as usual; never giving a second thought to the baby financial security blanket I crocheted for us.

I was silenced by his words and taken aback by his lack of fiduciary responsibility. As soon as the coast was clear, I wasted no time in sneaking upstairs to take another gander. However, I was unprepared for the shocking scene on that screen. I was dumbfounded, dismayed, and deflated to discover that the stock had taken a very unpleasant, ugly—large and costly—downward spiral.

Oh, what a financial fiasco. Feeling betrayed, I let my disappointment in my husband's lack of concern and attentiveness toward my stock be known. I pouted. I went into a funk. I ignored him. I tortured him. I reminded him daily with cutting remarks, with actions, and with inaction, how badly he'd behaved, how much we (me) had lost, how large a blow my ego had been dealt. It wasn't a pretty sight. I wasn't a pretty person.

Then paranoia got the best of me. I wondered if pure jealousy had caused the blunder. Had his egotistical envy prevented my windfall profits from becoming a reality? Here I was making an uninformed, uneducated stock picks based solely on woman's intuition, and they were winners. My husband studies and studies and runs chart after chart before he buys. I was in the winner's circle. He was on the sidelines watching. His ego couldn't let me be right! Time and again he'd gone against my advice, only to end up on the losing end of a stock transaction. Could it be that the green monster was alive and well, invaded my husband and taken up residency in his inner being? Was the male ego so fragile that it had prompted him to ignore my victory and sacrifice our monetary gains? Will I ever know? It was such a sad predicament.

Bearing the Big H

Under the influence of drugs and unable to climb the stairs to do my own monitoring, I had been defenseless, solely at my husband's mercy. This may sound dramatic, but it was really traumatic.

Although images of large clubs and baseball bats raced through my mind, part of me realized I was in a very precarious hormonal condition. Still, I wondered if the stock market could be used as grounds for divorce—or justifiable homicide. I was certain that a jury, given the circumstances of a hormonal rampage prompted by a husband's lack of fiscal responsibility, would have found me not guilty—at least by reason of hormonal instability.

Fortunately for him, I was able to contain myself and get a grip. I knew better than to push the point on this issue, so I silently stewed. Quietly and privately, alone every day after he left for work, the feelings would engulf me. I prepared a banquet of emotional entrees and then sampled each one: anger, depression, jealousy, revenge, sadness, regret, and loss. Late at night, once he was fast asleep, the feelings would surface again. I would succumb, fuming and stewing into the wee hours of morning. So sue me, I was ANGRY. What can I say? My friends knew it, my family knew; and had my husband cared to notice, he would have known it too.

I swear I tried to let it go. For the sake of our marriage, I tried not to vent my anger. But like any normal woman, I had to vent or I would explode, or implode, and I didn't know which would be worse.

So I vented to safe sources, narrating the nasty story to others near and dear to me. But my wisdom-wielding friends always came up with less-than-sympathetic comments like, "Fortunes come and go, but love lasts forever."

Oh, gag me with a spoon! I thought. Let's design wallpaper with that inscription on it and hang it throughout our entire house.

Finally the pressure built and I had to needle my husband one last time, shame him into submission, make certain he learned his lesson once and for all and would never do something like this again. So I mentioned my stock market-picks one more time and the fact that his irresponsible behavior caused a private stock market crash in our profits.

Very kindly, lovingly and oh-so sincerely my husband responded, "I am sorry that I was unable to keep a closer watch over our stocks, but I had more important things on my mind."

"Oh yeah, like what? What could possibly be more important than our financial future? Some minute matter at the office, I suppose?"I shot back at him, waiting for a full-blown fight, and the opportunity to totally dispense with all the vile that had built up inside me.

"Nothing," he replied dejectedly.

Damn! I just hate it when that happens. A man making sense and bringing me to my knees. Whether he was referring to his demanding work schedule, my surgery and/or recovery or a combination of it all, I will never know. And I wasn't stupid enough to ask. He was working eight to ten hours per day, even on weekends, coming home, waiting on me hand and foot, listening to me bark orders at him, doing the honey-do list I created each and every day, taking care of all the household chores and yard work, as well as walking the dogs.

In addition to all the work, he was also my personal sounding board, target for my frustration-induced daggers. Yet he managed to remain my constant companion no matter how difficult I made it. And he did it with grace, without uttering one complaint. Through it all, through all I had dished out to him, he'd managed to do what I had failed to do—determine what is important, focus on the positive, and let go of all the rest.

In that one short response my spouse had said a mouthful. That one word, coupled with his lack of words silenced me to tears. At that moment I was overcome with gratitude for the gift I'd been given in him. And realized all the rest was truly insignificant.

EIGHT

No Laughing Matter

It's funny how things happen in life. During recovery, the less *do-do* happens the better. But this was not the case during my recuperation. Anything that could bother me seemed drawn to me, from the tiniest to the tremendous, like a magnet to steel.

It all started with the case of the persistent plume. I had heard of it but never experienced it. Of course, it was not until this operation that a feather decided to take up residency in the middle of my throat. And I do mean residency. Not one day or two or three, but for many days this irritating tickle terrorized my throat—and me with it.

Any other time, one good, hard cough would have cured it, but I knew that would not be wise in my current condition. However, an involuntary reflex kept causing me to cough in an attempt to free the thing from its grip on my tonsils. It was not by choice, I assure you, that I even attempted to cough, for I knew that type of motion would cause a whole lot of commotion, more specifically—pain. I didn't need to experience it to know better than to try it.

But I was just plain desperate. The stubborn quill would not quit. So I had to do what I had to do to rid my throat of the annoyance. It was time to attempt the eradication. In preparation, I positioned my stabilizing pillow tightly against the sensitive and tender tummy area. Next, I tightly wrapped both arms around my feather-filled friend, closed my eyes and prayed. Leaning forward I managed a little cough. Uhhkkkk. First there was a little light groaning sound, somewhere between a grunt and a cough. As hard as I tried that was all that came out.

Can't be too careful was my thinking here. Lets not be a hero. But that tactic did little to correct the situation. I made another attempt, this time slightly harder and somewhat more forceful. Nothing. I coughed again, and again. I could tell at this point relief was not going to be easy, or quick. Frustrated and sore, I gave up. However, next day the foe still lingered in my larynx.

For days I was victim to this pain in the . . . throat. For the longest time I coughed, trying to dispel it without success, my abdomen in agony with each attempt. The coughing took its toll on me, but the feather was unscathed. Each day the soreness increased from the expulsion exercises. Finally, after I accepted the fact that it might be a long and brutal battle, the enemy retreated and left me in peace. Just like that, as quietly as the feather found its way in, it miraculously floated back out.

Many other recovery-threatening events served to keep me on my toes. Before surgery, I loved to sneeze. A good, loud sneeze always felt good to me. It was an inner release, my respiratory system ridding itself of all foreign matter, a cleansing of sorts. There was never a sneeze when I didn't feel sooo much better afterwards. But again that was then and this was now.

While fighting the feather, I was thankful that at least I had been sneeze-free, so far. Nothing lasts forever, and this was unfortunately the case with my sneezing. I felt it coming. I had feared the moment. I knew it would happen eventually, and when it did my tummy would pay the ultimate price.

There was a warning of sorts, that familiar itchy feeling in my nose. Oh, I panicked! Then took precautions and prepared myself. Quickly I grabbed for my pillow, using it as a brace by pressing it snugly against my stomach. I assumed the "defensive position," bringing my knees up to my chest and hugging them tightly. I knew danger, and pain, was imminent.

In my case, sneezes presented quite a threat. My sneezes have never been delicate or reflective of my quiet demeanor, or my small statue. No, not my sneezes. I always thought the louder the better. I never hamper them by trying to contain them. They are always big, bold, sonic booms that could probably be heard a block away. Such a large, loud production for such a petite person. I didn't know how to do this any other way.

Now that the sneeze was in motion and coming out, there was no stopping it. Nervously, I waited, and braced.

AAAAAAAACHOOOOOOOOOOOOOOOO! First the

deafening noise . . . and then the physical repercussion, the needle-sharp pain ricocheting from nerve to nerve the entire length of my body. Reflexively, I let out a blood-curdling scream.

OOOUCCCHHHHHHH! The yell shook the house.

I was home alone so I didn't scare anyone that I knew of. But looking around, I realized the windows in the front of the house were wide open (as was my mouth). I slid deep into the love seat, out of sight, just in case a neighbor heard the scream and came rushing to rescue me from the certain horror that would produce such a scream. I waited, in hiding; fortunately no one came.

I am not much for four-letter words of the cussing type, although there are instances when nothing else quite seems appropriate. If ever there was an occasion, this was it. However my cries consisted of only one four-letter word: ouch.

Over the next two months whether in private or in public, the routine was the same whenever a sneeze approached. I had it down pat. First was the tummy support, then the achoo followed with a cry of ouch! It was bad enough in the privacy of my home; but once I began to venture out in public this sneezing spectacle became a real attention-getter.

Fear and pain taught me to thwart my sneezes as best I could. I longed for the days when I would once again able to rattle the roof with my sneezes and unleash my heart's desire without rushing for a pillow to hug. But I chalked it up to just another healing hindrance along the rough and rocky recovery road.

However, the worst experience during recovery was the lack of laughter. The person (and I use that term loosely) who started the ugly rumor about laughter being medicinal obviously never had their gut held together by strips of adhesive tape and a few pieces of flimsy string. I am here to testify that humor under these circumstances is far worse than any torture I ever imagined. It took only the first encounter with my comical brother to learn that nothing hurts like laughter in the wake of the Big H.

Sibling rivalry was always at work where my younger brother and I are concerned. Therefore, it came as no surprise that he would use my frail condition as ammunition and unload on me. I think he made the 500-mile journey north during my recovery just so he could personally smother his sister with his "unique" kind of brotherly love.

He wasted no time in attacking his defenseless sister. Whether in person or on the telephone, his greeting was always the same.

"Hi, Novary," he ribbed.

What can I say, other than my younger brother is a sick (but lovable) person with a warped sense of humor? He's a frustrated comedian who never attained stardom and fame. Those of us in his immediate family are stuck with being the targets of his sick sense of humor.

It was not enough that he called me by his new pet name of Novary. No, he had to go the distance, finding something comical in everything around us, even those things void of humor to the rest of us.

He came to visit, not to keep me company, but for torture. Without fail, he would cause me to giggle, then grunt and gasp in pain. This, in turn, would cause him laughter. I believe his warped sense of humor may also be a family trait. My husband has, on occasion, accused me of having this same flaw.

Sometimes during his visits, we'd take his comedy routines outdoors. I was always on pins and needles, waiting for his antics to commence. Being the *good son* that he is, he never failed in his attempts to humor me. Using whatever props available, his comedy act would commence. During one show he discovered a long, broken stem from my split-leaf philodendron. Of all things to use as his accomplice on this occasion he choose a plant and a pet. Using the stem as a pointer, he acted as a dog trainer.

He tapped her with the stem and told her to sit. Being a not-so-good, not-so-obedient dog, she knows only one command, which happens to be sit. So she obliged him. Once she had obediently assumed her position, she then instinctively rolled over on her back with all four paws in the air. This is her favorite *rub my tummy, please* position.

The comedian then took advantage of her new position and barked another command at her, literally barking the command in his imitation of Scooby Doo's human/dog-like voice.

"Roll over," he commanded.

She just laid there on her back looking up at him with her innocent, loving eyes. Then like a prisoner trying for a quick escape, she got up and bolted.

With stem in hand, he chased her around the yard all the while yelling commands and barking orders in his authoritarian, dog-training tone of voice. Watching the two of them was the funniest thing I had seen since before surgery. Of course, this was the opinion of a hormone-deprived, postoperative convalescent. Perhaps you would have had to witness the scene to fully appreciate the moment.

I tried not to laugh, but I couldn't stop the giggles. It was so funny that it hurt. The sight of the two of them acting like idiots, running wildly around the yard, caused me great pain. So much so that I didn't want my brother to come visit anymore, for I sensed he was getting a sick pleasure out of making me laugh. It was, I'm sure, revenge for all the sibling childhood abuses I inflicted upon him.

Always he would leave and my laughter-void life would return. It may have been better physically, but worse emotionally. It struck me as sad that the one thing that brings so much joy, a good, belly-tickling laugh, could deliver such gut-wrenching pain. By far the hardest thing for me to deal with during recovery was the lack of laughter. And it lingered the longest. Three months after surgery, when all the other pains had dissipated, laughter still hurt.

During this time, there was no merry in merriment. Very quickly I grew tired of this lack of laughter. As if to fill the void in my life, a new, strange sense of humor emerged. Despite the pain, I would often perceive hysterically funny things that were really not that funny.

Early one morning I was sitting on the patio when a turtle slowly came crawling across the lawn. Curious about his destination, I watched as he sluggishly maneuvered from one end of the yard to the other. Then the purpose of his trip became apparent. It was a rendezvous with a turtle of the opposite sex! Before my very eyes, with little ado, the two did what turtles do to make baby turtles. I was upset that the male had not courted her more, brought her an insect for dinner. No, he just did his business and then left her. Another one-night stand, another notch on his shell.

Then it happened my sense of humor kicked in. I just had to tell someone about the steamy scenario in our backyard. So I called my husband.

"You wouldn't believe what these two turtles are doing right here in our backyard in front of God and me," I relayed the National Geographic moment. "And I don't think the man turtle treated the woman turtle very nicely."

"How do you know which is which?"

"Because the female is the one with a *glow* about her, and the male is the one sitting back smoking a cigarette."

I could barely get the words out through my laughter. I held the phone with one hand and clinched my stomach with the other. Although it hurt like heck, the giggles kept on coming. So silly, yet so funny—if only to me.

Unfortunately, my newfound sense of humor did not stop there. Soon after my homecoming my mate noticed the grass needed to be mowed. Playing nurse had taken its toll on the yard work. The tall grass outside was waving to him, signaling he had ignored his outside chores long enough. He left me horizontal on the sofa with sweet parting words.

"If you need me while I'm outside, I'll have my pager on, so just use the phone and page me. That way you won't have to get up."

Because he would be unable to hear the signal over the noise of the mower, he put the pager on vibrate mode. A tickle to his side would signal my summons.

I wasted no time in testing the system. The front door had barely closed when the fetching began. The first page was somewhat justified.

"Darling, would you please hand me the remote control over there on the coffee table. I need to change the channel, and can't reach it."

He graciously handed me the control, kissed me on the forehead, and headed outdoors, back to the waiting lawn mower.

It was a little spell later when he was vibrated again. He took the second beckoning with a grain of salt. However, the third page in less than one hour brought not my husband, but a small scowl as well. The fourth was to be my last call, as he came in with a roar and an outright ugly, contorted expression on his face.

"This better be really important," he barked at me, obviously holding back what he really wanted to say.

Very sweetly I answered. "Yeah, it is. I wanted a kiss and to tell you I love you."

He didn't say so, in words anyway, but I sensed he was *very* irate. He left without even a little peck on the cheek. He made only one departing comment as he slammed the door behind him, "I'm leaving my pager inside!"

Bored, and bound to the sofa, I called my mother to narrate the story to her. One by one, I described the vexations I had inflicted upon my poor spouse. The more I spoke, the funnier it got. (There it is, that twisted sense of humor I referred to earlier, that infamous family trait). Finally I broke out in full-fledged, roaring laughter.

Only one thing could have possibly been more painful than that laughter: The consequences if my other half had overheard me telling the story to his beloved mother-in-law.

It was the strangest thing I had ever experienced. Everything and everyone made me want to laugh, from simple human happenings to silly sitcoms.

I don't indulge much in television; for the most part I feel it's a waste of time. The older I get, the worse programs become, the less they appeal to me. So my favorites are mostly from the past.

I always liked the television show *Coach*. It was one of the very few sitcoms I watched religiously. I bet I saw every episode. With a television in our bedroom and no early morning appointments or wake-up calls, I could indulge in the luxury of staying up into the wee hours and watching late-night television during recovery.

When my husband married me he had visions of grandeur dancing inside his head, I just know it. My silly night owl of a husband equated marrying a younger woman with having more time for *night things*. Oh, that silly man! It was a real shocker when the truth came out, on our wedding night of all times. I was fast asleep before the lights were even out. And things didn't improve much after our honeymoon. As a matter of fact, he has grown accustomed to tucking me into bed before retreating to the living room to watch the ten o'clock news.

So for a woman used to being in bed, and asleep, by 10 p.m. this staying up past midnight and still getting in eight hours of sleep was indeed a luxury. I indulged in it to the max, watching every possible rerun of *Coach* that I could. This night, this episode seemed like the funniest I had ever seen—or rather, seen again. With a pillow pressed firmly against my stomach, I tried to suppress the laughter as I foolishly watched on.

As the show continued and giggles gushed forth, I tried every trick in the book to keep the laughter from tearing my stomach and stitches apart. In desperation, I searched for any hint of sadness in the events unfolding on the screen. However, it was just hilarious, at least in my state of mind. The coach and his assistant had gone to the ends of the earth to recruit a promising player. On their treacherous trek they camped in the cold wilderness, rode a raft down some perilous rapids, survived an avalanche, and journeyed high into the mountains via donkeys. They even witnessed some kids kicking what was described as goat heads. All this in an attempt to recruit this place kicker living high in a mountainous, remote part of the world.

Surviving the life-threatening adventure, the coach and assistant coach arrived at the talented place kicker's home just in time to witness him signing a contract with Lou Holtz, who beat the coaches to the dotted line because he had traveled by helicopter. I was in stitches the whole thirty minutes; fortunately my stitches withstood it all.

Enough was enough. The humor had to be hampered; it was taking its toll on my tummy. I was sore, and the source had to cease. Soon I learned to take precautions to prevent any more laughter. On occasions when we would go to my mother's house for Sunday dinner, I prepared myself for any assault by my family's sick sense of humor. Pillow at stomach, I found myself quickly leaving the dinner table at the very first hint of humor. I would walk out of earshot to the safety of silence.

As I learned to control my environment and dodge danger, my family, and yes, even my friends, learned that laughter was a method to control me. My husband found the threat of a tickle a promising source of behavior modification. As always, my brother was relentless and left no shots unfired. And my friends schemed ways to make me suffer at the hands of a joke.

Although time may cure everything, I must warn patients that laughter was the last to be impacted by the passage of time. Four months after bearing the Big H, my life was finally returning to some semblance of normalcy. I could walk two miles, and did so daily. But a giggle, a small belly laugh, half a chuckle would still send me reeling. I loved, and longed for, the return of laughter in my life. Not only was this the longest part of recovery, but for me, it was also the worst part of recovery. Life without laughter is merely an existence.

NINE

The Socking Truth

While lounging around one afternoon a strange thought occurred to me—how little I really know. No, not about everything, just one thing in particular. My operation! At the time of surgery, I wasn't interested in anything but getting the scalpel slicing. Nothing but that one thing mattered to me. I wanted relief and, at that point, any form relief took was all right with me.

I did not subject my physician to a preoperative interrogation. I should have drilled him endlessly beforehand, but I didn't. So, I wasn't privy to the details of the procedure. For instance, I did not know exactly which of my parts had been removed, or in what order. More importantly, I didn't know what was left by the wayside inside. I wondered if those remnants were just left hanging around or were tied down. Were they attached to some kind of anchor organ? If so, how? So many questions left unanswered.

It was only now, after all was said and done, that my curiosity got the best of me. I guess it was the reporter in me. For whatever reason, I craved all the gory details of the demise of my female anatomy.

However, my curiosity would have to linger until I could quiz the one who did the dastardly deed. I knew it wouldn't be long before I would see that crazy surgeon of mine. My first postoperative visit was fast approaching. It was scheduled for just two weeks after the Big H.

Sure enough, like clockwork, the big day arrived. After being cooped up in the house for fourteen days, I was actually looking forward to getting out and about, if even for a trip to the doctor's office. I did the usual things one would expect when trying to transform from a pale, sickly parasite to a queen bee. Surprisingly, I remembered how to apply makeup. However, there wasn't enough makeup in my house or, indeed, the entire cosmetic market to adequately manage this task.

It was useless and I was not in the mood to challenge my abilities in this matter. I was still a little weak, so I opted to save my strength for the trip. After applying a smidgen of blush, I donned my masking muumuu. I was ready to tackle the trip, that same grueling 80-mile round-trip, over those same agonizing bumpy roads. I shuddered at the thought of all the jolting and jiggling along that semi-paved, pot-hole-riddled washboard. But soon my focus shifted from the ride to the reason.

I looked down at the twelve strips of white tape adhering to my *very* fresh incision. I feared this was the day! The day those sticky pieces of material would be ripped from my body, and my life. Would pieces of me, my skin, and hair go with them? And how badly would it hurt? The same area that once was shaven bare was now host to a forest of newly sprouted pubic hair, proudly popping through that same adhesive. Just the thought of all the ridding and ripping made me worry about the impending visit. My facial expression changed. I glanced in the mirror before me, and staring back at me was the fretting frightened, wrinkled face of a Shar-Pei.

This promised to be a long day. Besides the anticipation over my appointment, my hormoneless state was beginning to take its toll. I was out-of-whack and probably out of control, if the truth were known. My moods were on a downward spiral, and the Ms. Hyde persona was appearing more often than not. In fact, the sweet and caring Dr. Jekyll was AWOL.

Being not only a witness, but also the main victim, of this unpleasant and terrifying transformation was my poor hubby. For two weeks he had been my personal punching bag and the target of my pointed tongue. I didn't really know if all this unpleasant behavior was a result of my recovery, the absence of hormones, or just the nasty side of my personality rearing its ugly head. Regardless of the reason, my spouse bore the brunt of it. Now, after all that he had endured, he was volunteering to be the one to drive me to and from the doctor's office. What a masochist! What a brave soul! Imagine being locked inside the confines of an automobile for a two-hour round trip with an out-of-sync spouse. I on the other hand was in hog heaven, for it produced a captive, audience—victim.

The trip was bearable (at least to me), thanks in part to my peace-provoking pain pills that made everything seem so lovely. The trip, I thought, went rather quickly. It was a scene straight out of the movies, my husband *Driving Ms. Daisy* and me driving him nuts. Luckily, before things got too ugly between the pilot and the commander-in-chief, we arrived at the doctor's office.

Although emotionally damaged during the drive, my spouse remained thoughtful and accommodating letting me out in front of the office so I wouldn't have to walk the distance of the parking lot. I was thankful he didn't just open the door as he sped by the building and push me out onto the pavement. At this point, he probably figured he had too much time, energy, money, and patience invested in me.

Once inside, I wasted no time in spreading my *joy* around to the office, to the staff. I was anxious to expel my venom on a new victim—a loving soul that wasn't four-legged or married to me. The magazines in an ob-gyn's office leave a lot to be desired unless you are planning, expecting, delivering, or growing children. With slim pickings, I skimmed through the appropriate periodicals in no time at all and was left to climb the walls and complain. I sat and sighed in a volume I was certain could be heard by the office staff. Had I been on the other side of that sliding glass panel, I would have slammed it shut after the first five minutes of the huffing and puffing sounds.

It is one thing for a doctor to run behind schedule, but quite another to keep an estrogen-estranged, looney lady sitting in a waiting room full of pregnant women! They all looked and acted identical—the same sickening grin on their faces, clutching their "tinkle cups" with one hand rubbing their protruding stomach with the other while whispering sweet things into the ear of the proud papas-to-be sitting smugly nearby. Yuck! How precious it all was. I sat there next to my verbally-abused, downtrodden husband, and rubbed my stitches that held my swollen and protruding tummy together. All the while I cussed not one, but two, loud sneezes.

I may be his patient, but a patient person I am not. It is one of my biggest faults. I don't like to wait anywhere, for anything or anyone. I have been known to drive thirty minutes out of my way so as not to wait five or ten minutes in traffic. This is in direct conflict with my husband. A true engineer, he is precise, methodical and oh-so careful and correct in all he does. He will take three hours to do something that it only takes me ten minutes to accomplish. Of course, he always has the same excuse for his snail-pace, perfectionist personality.

"I like to do things the correct way the first time and then it doesn't ever have to be done over again," he claims repeatedly whenever I nag him about finishing a household job—in my lifetime.

I truly believe, as I have told him, that God brought us together so I could learn patience and he could learn tolerance. Obviously we both have a whole lot of learning left to do.

Finally, after fifty minutes, a full 5-0, I was moved from the outer waiting room to a private exam (waiting) room. I am sure they didn't want my behavior to induce anyone's labor. The nurse took my blood pressure, which surely would send the mercury shattering from its glass gauge. However, she assured me that, although I was hot, I was not overheated as far as her medical instruments were concerned. I explained my adhesive apprehension.

"Oh, don't worry. It won't hurt; but if you are really upset about it, the tape doesn't have to come off this visit. It can wait until your next appointment in two weeks," she sympathetically said. This was, indeed, music to my ears.

Like me, the nurse had also been through the Big H. Therefore, she could understand, empathize, and relate more than a man, or a male physician. She stayed and visited with me awhile, relaying her postoperative experiences and offering friendly, female advice. The doctor had set *relative* recovery at six weeks, the point at which I could resume most normal activities. But my hysterectomy cohort gave a more realistic recovery schedule than that of her gender-flawed boss.

According to the nurse's experience, it was eight to twelve weeks before normal activity resumes. Not wanting to know what normal encompasses, I left it alone. Ignorance is bliss. She did say that for the first six months, and I repeat, six months, she was exhausted.

"I was so tired I could hardly function," she recounted. "You just don't fully realize the strain your body undergoes with this surgery." She continued in terms I had no problem understanding, terms that sent chills down my spine and raised red, flying flags.

"Honey, if you knew what goes on during a hysterectomy, you would be shocked. They just get in there, move things around and then take things out of your body," she so delicately divulged. "It will take a long time for your body to heal completely."

Oh, how soothing her words of comfort. NOT! I felt better already, and I hadn't even seen the doctor yet.

With those *tender* descriptive parting words, she handed me the gown and left the room, claiming the doctor would be in soon. Yeah, right! Heard that before. There I lay, horizontal on a hard, cold half of a table with my feet dangling over the end, bare-butt but for the designer tissue paper smock that "ties in back." Now I was nervous and comfy, too.

To entertain patients in this position, the ceiling had been decorated with posters befitting an obstetrician's office. High above me was a montage of rug rats. There were posters and pictures of all types, colors, shapes and sizes of kids— babies in flower pots, babies wearing diapers, babies with bears, babies, babies, everywhere were babies. I was afraid it was about to rain babies. The images were suffocating me when the door finally opened.

No doubt about it, there was finally cause to cuss: The doctor had made his untimely entrance into the examining room. Earlier, my better (and wiser) other half warned me to resist the temptation of a temper tantrum.

"Baby, please, take my advice and wait until the exam is over before spouting off," he pleaded. "I don't think you want to upset the man who is about to remove the tape from your incisions and stitches. He could possibly cause you some additional discomfort."

Since when had I listened to, or actually followed his intelligent advice? However, I would learn my lesson this time; soon I would pay the price for not partaking in his wisdom. But then I have priorities. Venting and verbalizing were the only things on my mind the exact moment when *his majesty* waltzed into the exam room. Like an out-of-control semi-tractor trailer headed for the run-away lane, there was no stopping my sharp tongue until it hit its target, made its mark.

I started hassling the poor doc the second he hustled through the door. Not without cause: I had spent almost sixty full minutes tapping my toes and cooling my heels in various rooms. I struck with such speed there was no warning at all, not even time for the customary exchange of pleasantries between doctor and patient. The moment the door closed behind him he was waylaid.

"I can't believe you kept me waiting almost one whole hour. I mentioned that to my husband and he asked what was so unusual about an hour's wait in a doctor's office. My answer to him was it's me doing the waiting," I spewed at the doctor with a snarled-up lip and a puffed-out chest. But I wasn't finished.

"Last time a doctor kept me waiting forty-five minutes, I got up and walked out," I rambled on without catching my breath. I was on a roll.

"And I can't believe *you* would actually charge me a couple thousand dollars for the honor of removing my female organs. And don't you think that you should have at least one examining room without baby paraphernalia adorning the walls and the ceilings for those of us like me who are and will always remain childless because they just had their mother-making materials removed?" There, it was all said, and almost in one breath.

The doctor's eyes were as big as saucers by the time my ranting was completed. He simply covered his mouth with his hand and looked at my husband, who was crouched in the corner, his flushed face a tone somewhere between Rudolph red and flaming fuchsia.

"Wanna know how I'm doing?" my husband innocently asked the doctor.

"No need. You have my sympathy. How long has she been like this?" my physician asked as if I was invisible or deaf and mute. Perhaps he did not want to risk another rampage by addressing me directly.

"Either put her on hormones or put me on them," my

sympathetic spouse affectionately pleaded.

Well, needless to say, I was about to learn two valuable lessons. First always take (or at least carefully consider) husbandly advice, especially when it doubles as a warning. Second, never give a doctor a GOOD reason to be less than gentle with your sore, healing body.

The doctor must not have been privy to the nurse's and my plan of postponing the tape removal. Before I knew what was happening, his latex-gloved fingers were clutching the first in the row of little white stripes. He seized the moment—and the tape—as an opportunity to *rip* me back to reality. It was payback time. I could tell.

With sick pleasure, one by one, he quickly tore off each of the strips. I could hear the tape as it departed its temporary home built on a foundation of human flesh—my flesh, my sensitive and oh-so hurting skin!

RIPPPPPPPPPPPP. One gone and eleven more to go. RIPPPPPPPPPPPPP. Another one down. And so the grueling unveiling went on, and on, and on.

In rapid succession, the incision swiftly became unbandaged. Nothing but a huge, ugly, swollen, bright red ripple across the grain of my abdomen was left. Quickly, a row of rough bumps popped up, as if out of nowhere. The little pubic sprouts survived the attack and were immediately surrounded by a crimson, ugly rash outlining the exact location where the tape had been.

Certain he had done all that on purpose, I yelled, screamed, ranted, and raved, accusing him of being not only callous, but calculating. I got no sympathy however. My complaints regarding the manner, and speed, in which the painful procedure had been done, fell on deaf ears. Both my husband and my doctor (it is important to emphasize here, both of them are men) assured me this was the only way to go.

"Oh, no, it's far better to rip the tape off than to slowly remove it. It's less painful that way," the mad doctor tried to convince me.

Then his co-conspirator got into the act. "He is right, Honey. It does hurt less that way."

I was no fool. I knew better. There was surely an easier,

less painful, less traumatic and dramatic way to remove tape attached to a stitch-filled tummy. My preferred method involved moisture, soaking, time, and gentleness—slow and easy. I thought of an even better, more compassionate way to rid one's self of adhesive: The best scenario would be soaking in the bathtub and waiting until the tape tabs voluntarily departed the stomach, without force, in their own time, of their own accord. Now I will never know. I was robbed of the opportunity to reveal to the world the best, least painful, method of removing bandages.

Having my incision exposed, I felt naked and vulnerable. Before this moment no one had laid eyes on my full incision. The doctor then bent over my stomach to get a closer look.

"Not bad, you won't even be able to see this when it fades. Have you seen this?" he asked my husband, without my input, or permission.

He just put his handiwork on parade, as I lay flat on my back unable to get into their conversation. I didn't think my stomach and his stitching was worthy of such fanfare and display.

After the two had had their viewing, the doctor remembered that there was a person (namely, me) underneath the scar.

"By the way, I did not charge you for the removal of your organs. There was no charge for that," he told me.

"What? What are you talking about? We were billed for your surgical services and paid the price."

"It was not the surgery, it was sewing you up that cost you." he said. "Like pilots say, there is not a charge to fly a passenger overseas, it's the landing that costs."

Oh, how did I get so lucky to rate a physician who was also a frustrated comedian?

Finally the torture finished—or so I thought. There was one last matter to be addressed before I could dress. Having witnessed firsthand one of my hormonal rages, it was inevitable that the doctor would recommend HRT (hormone replacement therapy). The time had come. My fate was now sealed. The damage had been done and there was no turning back. My emotional instability and irritability were convincing factors that the time had arrived to prescribe some mood-altering, husband-soothing drugs, and the sooner the better.

The doctor didn't even ask my opinion on the subject;

he just pulled his prescription pad out of his pocket and sat down at the table. He began writing, paused and then stopped. Puzzled he looked at the nurse. She peered over his shoulder and read his scribble.

"No, she wants to be happy. Give her a real dozy of a dose," she smiled.

Therefore, at the urging of the nearby nurse, the doc prescribed not one, not one and a half, but two milligrams of hormones. I wondered if this was for my benefit or out of sympathy for my husband. He then gave me a sample of some *foreign* hormonal delivery system and explained the rules and regulations of its use. With it, I received a prescription for a year's supply of "harmony."

Suddenly my husband grabbed both the prescription and sample out of my hands. I looked at him puzzled.

"For safekeeping," he said with an ear-to-ear smile.

I was ready to rid myself of these two. I was outnumbered. I just wanted to dress, depart, and head back to the safety—and sanity—of my own home. Then I remembered my list of questions. Before doc left for safer ground, I stopped him.

"I know it may seem silly that I want to know now, after the fact, but exactly what did you do inside me, and how did you do it?"

He was very willing to describe in exact details how he cut me and gutted me. Using my abdomen as a backdrop, he demonstrated exactly how my uterus and other organs were taken from their home. Then, using a somewhat unique prop, he explained the location of the stitches inside me.

Like in most gynecologist examining rooms, the end of the table was adorned with the dreaded set of cold, hard, metal stirrups. In a futile attempt at a cleaver cover-up, some wise person (a woman, I am sure) had the bright idea to shroud the intimidating foot-holding, leg-spreading device with soft, fuzzy warming booties. My doctor's office was no different.

It was one of those socks that costarred with my doctor in the debut production of *How To Undo What Mother Nature Had Done*. With sock in hand, he began his narrative of what was removed and how my unmentionables were now all tied together.

"When we removed the uterus and ovaries, we pulled

the surrounding muscles apart, so as not to cut them," he explained eloquently.

" . . . Then we stitched the top of the vagina closed with absorbable sutures—like the seam of this sock. See here, your internal incision looks like this," he pointed to the toe of his sidekick prop.

Well, this sure gave me something to ponder. Images of stitched sock seams swirled in my head. Would my stitched vagina resemble the delicate threads of a nice expensive dress sock or be the broad and heavy-duty seam of an athletic sock? Was I a *Gold Toe* or a generic brand? At this point in my life, I didn't want to be the athletic type. I had just lost part of my womanhood. I wanted my seam stitching to be the feminine type, a seam fit for a pretty, delicate, fancy trouser sock. The doctor abruptly interrupted my daydreaming.

"And on your next visit I will examine the end of your internal sock to determine how the seam is doing," he smugly announced.

At that moment it was apparent that he really liked torturing me! Maybe not physically, but certainly psychologically.

The mere thought of him (or anything) being inserted inside my ever-so-tender, surgery-ravaged body sent chills down my spine, and escape plans through my mind. Skip the country, or at least the state . . . Don't make a follow-up appointment . . . Make the appointment and then get sick. Anything, but just stall for time, my body begged of me.

Paranoia set in and did cruel and unusual things to my mind, what little was left.

Cancel, reschedule, cancel, skip the country or at least the state. He won't come looking for me. He wouldn't hunt me down just to hurt me, would he?

Hurry! I had to get home. There was not a minute to waste. Time was of the essence. I had to get in gear. There were only two weeks to prepare, plan, and become physically fit for my great escape.

TEN

Patching Things Up

After waging war for two weeks, I had fallen in defeat. This surgery thing was making a defeatist out of me, and that was a hard pill for me to swallow. Now, after my brave attempt without hormones, I was forced to surrender to the appeals for peace from those around me. The pressure was so intense; I was left with no other choice. Those pitiful cries echoing in my ears day after day, night after night, accompanying the pathetic expressions on the faces of my husband, family and friends.

"Hormone replacement therapy, HRT, please, please. Get some hormones in your system so you will be tolerable again," they all pleaded.

No question about it. I was unbearable. Frankly, I was becoming insufferable even to myself. For the safety of those around me, the time had come for me to resort to hormone replacement treatment.

Honestly, I confess to being disappointed in my hormoneless stretch. Absent were the infamous night sweats and hot flashes of which I had heard so much about. I was curious to know what all the hullabaloo was about.

Of course, when it is 105 degrees outside it's hard to determine what is normal temperature-induced perspiration and what is hormonally-produced heat. Oh well, I may never know. Maybe the flashes and/or sweats will make a guest appearance sometime in my future. Then again, perhaps I have been spared those two hysterectomy hallmarks altogether.

No, say it isn't so! Life, maturity, and womanhood without night sweats and hot flashes, surely not. How would I and what could I contribute to my later convalescent conversations if spared these feminine phenomenons? What would I have to add to the daily crochet conversation when I am eighty or ninety years old and surrounded by my new (and used-up) nursing home girlfriends?

"Honey, do you remember all those terrible, restless nights when those nasty ol' night sweats came callin'? I remember it like it was yesterday. My husband used to just roll over and fall back to sleep, leavin' me to sweat all alone. Oh, those were the days. Remember them, Emma?"

"Sure, Charlotte, I barely remember, but it was them scorcher thangs that caused me all the trouble during my change of life. There was a catchy name for 'em. Give me a minute and maybe it'll come to me. It had to do with temperature or thermometers. Wait a minute, it's a comin' to me— warm spot, no. That ain't it. It was something like it, though. Hold on, I'll get it. Yeah, it was warm. No. It was hot, hot . . . rashes . . . flashes! That's what them thangs were. Red as a bing cherry I was when they came on. I am sure glad all them female fusses are over! Now if I could just get my plumbin' fixed I would be rarin' to go."

With nothing to add, I would be reduced to just sitting, knitting, and gritting. But there was plenty of time to worry about that later. Back to present and the matter at hand.

Being an inquisitive reporter, I asked my doctor before surgery why I should even consider HRT in the first place. I wanted the facts, just the facts, sir. What are the benefits? Why aren't the pros and cons ever discussed? What are the negatives and positives of hormone replacement therapy? Why isn't the ultimate choice of partaking in HRT given to the patient, instead of dictated by doctors? It seems like HRT is so routine it is rarely discussed as an option. It seems medically mandatory, a given that women should be on hormone replacement therapy once they undergo the Big H. Is prescribing HRT just standard operating procedure in the gynecological gamut of things? As I understand it, my case was somewhat rare in that I waited even a minute after leaving the operating table to begin *the therapy*.

From what I gathered, it is normal for a woman to start HRT as soon as surgery is complete, like that very same day. However, being a nonconformist, my doctor and I chose another course of action. We waited. Of course there was a medically sound reason for this action, or rather inaction. Prior to surgery, my gynecologist explained some doctors feel postponing hormones replacement therapy lessens the chance of endometriosis resurfacing. He did however add the caveat that this thinking and practice are questionable.

"But the choice is yours. If you want to wait a while, we can do that and begin HRT if life without it becomes unbearable," my doctor said before surgery. "The decision is entirely up to you."

I figured what the heck. I had never been one to follow the norm before. What harm could come of it anyway? I would wait as long as possible to introduce foreign agents into my system.

"Let's wait and see what happens," I made the decision on my own, without my spouse's knowledge or input.

The less he knew the better. He wouldn't be able to hang all my faults on yet another hormonal hook. For years, my hormones had been taking the fall for my less-than-cheery demeanor, while pain, the real culprit, usually skated scot-free.

Life without hormones couldn't be *that* bad. Nevertheless, I was losing a close friend, my crutch, and my excuse for all those many, many times during a month when my mood was less than tolerant, and tolerable. But it's said that one door doesn't close without a new one opening. This way I would have a new scapegoat. Part of me needed a little excuse insurance, just in case I emerged from surgery with the same old *challenging* personality.

"I'm sorry, but I can't help it, Honey. I know I am irrational and behaving like a beast, but remember my hormones are spiraling. I'm not on HRT you know."

The thought of having a backup excuse for inexcusable behavior was a real comfort to me. It was part of the reason, I opted to forego HRT, a rare decision, as I was about to discover.

I am sure my gynecologist was busy on discharge day (D-Day), otherwise tied up on the tee box, so another gynecologist was on rounds that weekend. It was, therefore, a total stranger to my case that came to sign the discharge papers.

Once inside my room, the doctor wasted no time in getting down to business. He began with what I assumed was the normal discharge line of questioning.

"You have started HRT and have that prescription, right?" he asked while scribbling on the hospital chart.

"No, I haven't started hormones yet. I am not on them."

Bewildered he asked, "Why not?.".

I explained the decision reached with my doctor. He looked across the room at my husband with raised eyebrows. Finally, seeming to choose his words carefully, he spoke.

"Well, postponing HRT is not widely practiced" he said. "While I do see some cases where endometriosis has returned after a hysterectomy, it is rare, and probably would happen with or without HRT."

Yet he didn't sway me. This just went to further prove my theory of *routinely* dispensing hormones. I wonder if it is a man thing, a sympathizing gesture from the brotherhood of male doctors to hysterectomy-surviving male spouses. A preventative measure aimed at paving the way or rather ensuring a smoother ride.

So why now, so early in the game, were we changing the course of action? What, I wondered, had caused the prompt (and what I viewed as a radical) reversal of physician's advice regarding the withholding of hormones. It might have been my most recent conversation (as I affectionately chose to call it) with the doctor, the one in which venom spewed forth during my postoperative office visit. That experience may have been what prompted his adamant order to begin HRT immediately. After that manic monologue, I'm surprised he didn't order an immediate intravenous dose.

However, having this wild imagination, I concocted another theory. It is plausible that my husband called the doctor in advance of our visit, pleading his case and begging for some relief. A covert conversation accompanied by the offer of a large bribe would have definitely sealed my fate. But the how and why no longer mattered. Help for us all came in the form of a patch. Not pills, but a patch, I say.

Like a sneaky woman going undercover to take a pregnancy test, it was in the privacy of the bathroom that I first got up-close and personal with my new sidekick. Literally, a sidekick, for this was not your run-of-the-mill pill delivery system. No way. My hormones were to be delivered the new and improved way, via the Twenty-first Century new millennium mode; the vogue, "invisible" way; via a patch, a round, sticky adhesive kind of patch, the kind that attaches to skin. Why a patch I didn't really know for sure. I did know, however, that I had paid for a month's supply of the annoying things and been given some free samples to boot. I am too frugal not to take advantage of the samples and get my money's worth out of the prescription.

Therefore, being an adventurous and modern type woman, I embarked on the patch pilgrimage. Besides, my doctor said that many of his patients prefer the patch. It is claimed that once the patch is applied to the skin, it is virtually invisible. Of course, it's probably those marketing maniacs that make this claim. What would they know, other than how to make life miserable (or more so) for menopausal women everywhere? But it didn't take long for me to dispute their claim.

Being a newcomer to this pharmaceutical process, I made certain to actually read and follow all the directions—a rare occurrence. Usually I am too impatient to waste time on something as trivial as reading directions. However, this did concern my physical health as well as my husband's mental well-being, so I couldn't be too careful.

Eager to see my *lifesaver* I quickly peeled open the protective foil packaging. Wow! I was not prepared for what was there—or rather was not there. It was so small, so unassuming. I studied the circular cellophane before me knowing that soon it would become an appendage. I touched it. I fondled it and pondered it. I held it up to the light looking intently into and through it. Like a beachcomber discovering a genie bottle, I rubbed it thinking maybe the magic powers would come forth and grant my wishes. No way! How in the world could this inconsequential disk carry out such a massive undertaking? Tell me it isn't true! My emotional stability, mental state, and marital status all hinged on this one small piece of flimsy film?

Dismissing my size-based prejudices, I continued in my quest for peace. Following the instructions to the letter, very carefully I peeled away the outer protective shield. Then, *with even and firm pressure*, I strategically applied the patch to the dictated area of my body. I waited for results. And the results were almost immediate: I became a living, walking, breathing lint trap.

Once the patch was in place, an icky, sticky adhesive

circle magically appeared around the outer perimeter. And this ring did not dissipate with the passage of time. Rather, it grew larger, darker, and stickier with each passing day. I was decorated with the same annoying goop that remains when price tags are removed. Just imagine how wonderful it is to have that same sticky substance stuck to your skin, purposely and semi-permanently.

It is surprising how many household objects are attracted to a patch that happens to be passing by. Things that are floating in the air, things hidden in blankets, things undetectable to the human eye—are all mysteriously drawn to the patch. In no time at all my sidekick became a household cleaning system.

At the end of the day, I would inspect the accumulated-particles. It was like throwing a fishing net out into the Gulf of Mexico and being filled with anticipation of discovering the variety of aquatic treasures soon to be reeled aboard. To a lesser degree, this patch provided the same experience, only instead of catching identifiable and edible fish, I was stuck with unidentifiable "floaties" of various shapes, sizes, and colors.

Not meaning to brag, but over time I became somewhat of an expert on the identification and habits of floaties. The balled blanket fluffies accumulate at a rapid rate, and that rate is dependent on various factors such as time, temperature, and volume. The cooler the temperature, the more a blanket is used, the more fuzzes attach. Likewise, the more one frequents the bed, the more susceptible she becomes to covers and their fuzzy by-products. So it just goes to reason, the more blankets piled on a bed, the more fuzzes become attached to the gooh of the patch.

I have two dogs and two cats, which wouldn't be relevant but for one important fact—their shedding critter coats. On those occasions when fluffies didn't fill the circle of goop, sweet little reminders of my shedding pets did. How beautiful the patch (and surrounding skin) became. Within a few days, the supposedly invisible patch was decorated with a rare collection of assorted household waste. Lovely! It was just gorgeous!

Unfortunately, each individual patch is good for one week, at which time it is replaced with a new one and the whole administering cycle begins again. Much to my chagrin, and disappointment, the stubborn little patch managed to stay in place after days of showering and scrubbing.

After seven days it's amazing how much becomes attached to the body via this magical, magnetic hormonal delivery system. The real trick comes with the removal of the clutter collection—without causing air bubbles to invade the inner zone (the little center of the patch containing *the* stuff that ever-important, mood-leveling, emotionally-stabilizing magical potion). Evidentially air bubbles can be detrimental to this delivery system

The next patch-related activity *searching for air bubbles* is best reserved for a time when the hostess is in the right mood, preferably a very good This task can be very ego-deflating, mind-altering, and mood-crushing.

Regretfully patches don't lie. Bubbles accentuate every bulge, every roll, every sag, and every wrinkle under every inch of the patch. Miraculously tiny, minute amounts of air some-how manage to squeeze between the patch and the fat and magically appear as air bubbles under the *invisible* patch. This is very alarming to women like me whose girlish figures have flattened, flabbed out and "fallen" victim to the aging process.

Now, I can't speak for anyone else, but in my own expe-rience I found that these air bubbles seemed to appear along fat creases. It is important to note that, according to the instruc-tions, there is only two places suitable for placement of the patch: "the upper quadrant of the buttocks or the abdomen."

This presented a real problem for me, since I have excess cell formation (a.k.a. cellulite, fat, and flab) on both my bottom and belly. No matter where I placed the patch, air bubbles inevitably appeared. It was a mystery to me and I began to wonder about the formation of this phenomenon. With noth-ing better to do in my less-than-robust condition, I decided to research this matter. Once the week was up, or the adhesive area surrounding the patch was filled up (whichever occurred first) another patch was applied. Then I waited and watched, intent on discovering how and why the air pockets appear.

Unfortunately, I found the answer. It is the unique jig-gling motion that causes bubbles to surface, the same jelly-type of jiggle that comes only from the movement of fat. It brought to mind that disgusting saying, it has to be jelly cuz jam don't shake like that. That kind of jiggle.

This was not only disgusting and annoying, but also counter-productive to my hormonal delivery system. How in the world can a person, namely a surgically menopausal woman, be expected to "level out" when her hormones are being delivered by a fat-accentuating, confidence-crushing, lint-collecting "invisible" device?

After only two days of riding on my fat-filled fanny, the bubbles invaded to a such a magnitude that I was forced to remove it. Talk about a real kick to the ego. At least it would no longer be a pain in the butt. It's hard to believe all this air bubble nonsense was really caused by my cellulite! On the other hand, I was pretty sure the proliferation of bubbles was directly proportional to the rate at which my fat cells were multiplying.

However, with samples yet to be applied, I wasn't ready to abandon this patch business altogether. I had an alternate plan—another location What was needed was a change of scenery. A new patch, a new location. That would make things all better. The tummy was now the target. Again I read the instructions. "To apply, peel the protective lining, position the patch and then apply pressure . . ." And obediently I complied. But only hours after applying pressure and sealing the patch securely on my stomach, I again found wrinkles in my cellophane. How revealing! How disgusting! If I had been searching for the location of fat folds, I would have consulted a mirror, thank you very much!

There was one bright spot in this whole ring thing. It provided an opportunity for my husband and me to revert to our past, to play a childhood game of sorts—at least a risqué rendition. Let the games begin! My husband affectionately applied at least one patch on my buttocks, mainly because he could manage a bird's-eye view of my hindquarters. Fortunately for my sake, that part of my anatomy is still located behind me and at least for now, is still out of my sight (however it's falling at a rapid rate). So instead of Pin the Tail on the Donkey, the patch and my butt played host to a round of *Glue the Patch on the Ass*.

It was real. It was fun, but it wasn't real fun—for me. So

I phoned my physician pleading for relief from my degrading new past times of lint picking and defaming my derriere. I begged him, "Pills. Please give me pills! Spare me any more agony at the hands of this insensitive patch."

Detecting a bit of desperation in my voice and not wanting to further disturb an already disturbed woman, he quickly agreed.

While the patch may be the preference of women, I am not such a brave soul. But I do have a few suggestions. Appropriate marketing of the patch is necessary. It should be renamed and advertised as the hormonal delivery *and cellulite identification* system. It should also contain the following warning label:

"Warning: Wearing the patch and discovering air bubbles may be hazardous and detrimental to one's mental (not to mention emotional) health and self-image. Women who are pleasantly plump (or more) should consult a shrink and a dietician before embarking on this potentially painful experience."

If, in the unlikely event women around the world drop the patch for the pills, all those disks won't be wasted. They can always be sold as dusting and lint removal systems.

ELEVEN

Hard Nut
To Crack

With little else to do while home and healing, I spent a great deal of time fretting, worrying and hallucinating about the impending second postoperative visit. I hadn't feared the surgery as much as I was dreading this appointment. Armed with consciousness-eliminating drugs, the surgery was a piece of cake, and pain was not part of the equation. This, however, was different: No drugs, no buffer, no pain prevention would be offered. The vivid picture he painted earlier regarding the purpose of the next visit—the a search for the "seam of the sock" scared my pants off.

My first postoperative visit had made me a little uneasy. Only fourteen short days after surgery, I was certain there wasn't much more pain he could inflict upon my traumatized anatomy at that point. But his rip-roaring fun with the tape removal proved me wrong.

Now after four weeks, a mere month of healing, I was heading back for another attempt. My diplomatic doctor had already primed me for the purpose of the pending appointment. Echoing through my mind, consuming my thoughts, and haunting my days and nights was his frightening forecast: "Next time I'm going to have to check the incision inside the vagina to make sure it's healing properly."

I had cringed at the thought then, and was still cringing. My jaw was as tight as a pair of heavily starched jeans, two sizes too small. Ouch, ooohhhhh, huh-uh, no, no way.

I feared my threshold for pain was about to be measured. That day, the examination day, was fast approaching. The thought of that metal contraption being inserted inside me to jack open my tender (very tender and very sore) war-torn female parts made me just a little crazy and a whole lot nervous. My abdomen was barely healed. My body, internally and externally, was still off-limits to both sight and touch. Now my doctor was going to invade, merely to assess the havoc he had previously wreaked on my poor body. I don't understand that logic. Of course, it was probably a man that decided a postoperative INTERNAL exam was necessary at the one-month point.

I thought of ways to warn him of the risk he was about to undertake. I had this picture of me lying on that noisy tissue-paper-covered, cold table, waiting, and waiting. Waiting and worrying. Oh how they love to make you wait. When the good ole doctor finally did make his grand entrance, I had my greeting all planned out in my head. The mere thought of it made me laugh, or at least snicker.

I would grab his private parts (of course being a *male* surgeon, he would still have his intact) and tighten my grip. Once I was sure I had his full attention then, with evil eyes and a scary scowl on my face, I would make my point. "Hurt me, Doc, and I will hurt you! Do I make myself clear?" But that seemed so extreme, so unladylike, so brazen and bold. It was so unlike me—and yet so tempting!

Screaming at the top of my lungs before he ever commenced torture was an option. As the blood-curdling sounds echoed throughout his office and infiltrated his patient-filled waiting room, I would explain it was just a small demonstration of what would happen if he hurt me. That, too, seemed inviting—and was manageable. I would certainly hold that thought.

Once the sweet images and possibilities began to swirl in my mind, the waltz would not stop. Soon another idea came to me, and then another. I thought about all my options and carefully plotted my course of action. In the end I opted for the subtle, yet stern approach.

As feared, the ominous day arrived—the moment of my second postoperative checkup, the intrusive, invasive one. Left with no viable escape route, I was forced to board *Better-Half Airlines* for the long journey to the dreaded appointment.

Having the take no prisoners attitude and loaded for bear, I was ready for what awaited me. I was armed. Hidden in my purse was a very deadly device.

Once in the doctor's office, my apprehension was apparent to everyone. I flinched every time the door to the waiting room opened. Perspiration flooded off my forehead with every strange name called. "Jackie Johnson." "Sandra Mooney." Wew! One of the lucky ones, I was still sitting, still safe.

Then it happened. The sound of a faintly familiar name sounded through the room. Instantly, I became paralyzed with fear. Like a frightened fawn hiding within the protective cover of tall grass, I sat camouflaged in the sea of surrounding females. I didn't move an inch. The nurse called my name again; only this time she spotted me.

She looked at me inquisitively. She just stood there in the doorway, staring at me, waiting for movement on my part. And move I finally did. My eyes (and the eyes only) moved slowly up from my magazine to meet her gaze. She waited. She glared.

"I am not going with you," I finally informed her.

Relief came over her face. "Well, I thought that was you. You had me thinking I had lost my mind or called the wrong name."

The nerve of that woman; how dare she! I couldn't believe that at a time like this, she was thinking about her own state of mind instead of mine. I always liked her, too. Well, scratch her off my Christmas card list.

My pity personality kicked into high gear. "No. He's gonna hurt me today, and I don't want to go with you!" I hadn't acted this childish even when I was a child.

"Oh, he is so gentle, and won't hurt you," she said as she quickly ushered me down the hall, out of earshot of the other patients.

Down the hall the nurse pushed me as my *Exorcist* behavior became more conspicuous. "Yeah right, has he ever done this to you?" I whined.

"No, he hasn't, but after having three children, a tubal ligation and a hysterectomy by another surgeon, I can assure you it won't hurt," she shot back. That did the trick. My whining stopped.

I must say I was a real trooper. And to my surprise, with the threat of bodily harm, my doctor was, indeed, gentle. I demanded no less and I let that be known as soon as he entered the examining room.

"Okay Doc, before you get started, I have something I want to show you." Very slowly, and with a great deal of drama, I reached into my purse and, ever so slowly, pulled out the bright, shiny silver nutcracker.

For full effect I squeezed the handles together. The clanking resonated from wall to wall, music to my ears. No explanation was needed, no words were necessary. My point had been made. The expression on his face let me know that he had gotten my message loud and clear.

But what the heck, I thought to myself, a few words just for dramatic emphasis would certainly add to the atmosphere.

"Just so we get this straight, you don't hurt me and I won't hurt you. So we don't want to hurt each other. Right?" Like a musician, I played my instrument as a special effect. With every word I spoke, the metallic clacking of my nutcrackers sounded, reverberating loudly.

With that show of force, the exam commenced. And, as quickly as it began, the inspection was finished. I felt as if I had been to an auto mechanic. There was the usual pressure of being cranked opened with a tire jack. The discomfort of having a cold, gooey lubrication job was the usual *happy* occasion. I was checked from bumper to bumper, in a very gentle manner. When it was all said and done, I was happy to report there was no more discomfort than that of the annual regimen.

Whether the doctor took heed of my warning and took that little show-and-tell threat serious or whether he really is always gentle, I honestly don't know.

However, this adventure did give me one great entrepreneurial idea. If, heaven forbid, I don't make it as an author, I can always set up a concession stand outside my gynecologist's office and sell nutcrackers to all his patients—with the following label attached: This nutcracker stunt is dangerous and should be attempted only by those certifiable. It should not be attempted at home, or in just any doctor's office. Improper use may be dangerous to a patient-doctor relationship and may result in permanent, irreversible damage—to one or more parties.

TWELVE

A Hairy Experience

There is one thing about womanhood I detest more than most, (and there are certainly several from which to choose). However, this particular one is genderly unfair shaving! For the life of me I can't figure out why women shave. It seems like we shave everything. Relatively speaking, compared to our male counterparts, we do shave everything. We shave so much that we are forced to shave so often.

Pre-puberty, I actually wanted to start shaving, to partake in this mature *privilege*. Little did I know then that this so-called rite of passage would eventually plague the remainder of my life.

My mother tried to warn me, but being a know-it-all teenager, I gingerly dismissed her motherly advice. I begged often and early to partake in this womanly ritual—long before the hairs had fully sprouted.

"Please, Mom, let me shave, just my underarms, just once. Please, please, please. There can't be any real harm in it," her silly adolescent child would reason and plead nonstop.

The begging became a weekly tradition from the time my first downy hairs appeared (only to me and my magnifying glass) until they became faintly visible to the human eye. On a routine basis, I would take my case (and my underarms) to mom for inspection. Yet she needed more convincing signs than a few straggling stray sprigs.

The hair on my legs was a different story altogether. I was born with those hairy things. I am sure I looked like a pale baby chimp right out of my mother's womb. The story is the same for my forearms. The hair there is still growing; and at my ripe old age it has now become almost long enough to braid. I was one of those unfortunate kids whose hairy arms were targeted by schoolyard bullies. The fur-covered things could be spotted miles away. And it never failed that when they were detected, torture was not far behind. The big kids would furiously rub my fuzz with the palms of their hands in a circular motion until knots appeared. I was then left with the painful task of picking them out, one clump at a time. My skin ached with each matted knot I plucked from my epidermis.

So my deep determination to shave was rooted in my childhood, and I was relentless in pursuing the pleasure of ridding myself of all possible fuzz. I never gave up the fight with mom. Figuring I had one leg up on her, yet another approach was tried. When she axed the underarm shaving week after week, I took my fine-feathered legs to her and pleaded my pitiful case, the newly revised version.

"Mom, how would you like to go out in shorts or even worse, a bathing suit and have everyone stare at your hairy legs?"

She would strain to see the little, transparent pinfeather growth on my legs. Shaking her head, rolling her eyeballs upward, she would then disgustingly dismiss my overly anxious teenage ways.

I held out as long as humanly possible for a headstrong and impulsive adolescent. Nonetheless, when a razor was discovered lurking in the corner of the medicine cabinet, I took matters into my own hands. Defying authority, I took my first step down the groomed path of adult life, without permission. With razor in hand, I found the shaving cream and waited for the house to empty. As soon as mom left the house for the grocery store, I became a rebellious, but clean-shaven, teenager.

My hands were shaking so badly during that first attempt, I was surprised I didn't cut an artery or amputate a toe on the long way down my shin. It was fun and I loved every passing swath I made through the shaving cream. I even managed to finish both legs without getting caught and without inflicting any wounds requiring medical care.

Despite what anyone else might say, the shaven legs vastly improved my looks, and self-image. However, I would have to hide the endeavor or suffer my mother's wrath for disobeying her. My scrawny, shaven legs went unnoticed by everyone but me. I admired them constantly and derived real pleasure from rubbing my hand over my clean-shaven, baby-butt-smooth legs.

My attitude changed with my grown-up look. The shy girl gave way to a confident, proud, stuck-up kid. I had what my girlfriends only dreamed of: shaven legs! After swearing each and every one of them to secrecy, I found pleasure in unveiling my new and improved adult legs to them all. And then rubbing their noses in it, or at least their hands over them.

My secret remained just that and my mother never discovered my teenage shenanigans, until I was much, much older, way too big to be spanked and living too far away to be grounded. It was the grounding I dreaded most. I was the only one of the kids in our family that was ever grounded. It wasn't because I was more unruly than the others, or my rebellion any worse. It was only the order of things. My older sibling was too old to ground (or so I was told) and my younger brother was the baby of the family and, as such, a "protected species."

Oddly enough, I was finally given permission to shave once I quit hounding my mother. It was one of those mother-daughter moments. I was sitting in my bedroom when mom knocked on the door. She came in and sat down beside me, clutching a beautifully wrapped package in her hand.

"What is that?" I rudely asked before she had a chance to speak. Presents took precedence over politeness.

"I have something for you, something I think you have been waiting for," she said handing me the gift. I was clueless as to its contents.

Within seconds the wrapping ripped, was tossed to the floor and the box opened. There inside was every teenage girl's dream—an electric razor. I was so amazed that she had given in, in such a grandiose manner. Then a wave of guilt and shame engulfed me.

Having defied her and sneaking around, I robbed my mother of one of those mother-daughter bonding occasions, the first shave. So I did what comes natural to all sneaks, I played along, admitted nothing. Not so much to save my own hide, but to salvage the moment for mom.

It worked and the precious bond was created—a bond, which years later would come back to haunt my mother. All grown-up a question of the personal sort arose, and I didn't know where to go for an answer. It was too personal even for a best friend, so I turned to mom. After all, it was her duty as a mother.

My pubic hair has only experienced preoperative procedural shavings. So I've never really known proper pubic hair protocol. It just grows at will.

This let-go-to-grow attitude of mine never presented a problem for me. Now my gynecologist may have a different opinion of that. Exam after exam, I've expected him to make a comment while trying to find the forest through the trees. I am waiting (and growing on) until the appointment when he hands me a barrette or a rubber band and says, "Here, get that stuff out of my way."

Before that embarrassing moment occurs, I thought I'd seek an opinion as to proper pubic procedure.

While driving to the store one day, I blindsided mom with this personal line of questioning. "Mom, do you shave your pubic hair?"

The ensuing silence was so loud it was deafening. The only things more unnerving were her bulging eyes and her dropped jaw.

"Why in the world are you asking me a question like that?" she asked as if we were not, nor had ever been, a mother-daughter duo. I explained my curiosity over the matter and my search for the proper hair length.

She cleared her throat several times and finally brushed my question, and me, off by curtly saying, "I don't know." End of subject! End of conversation!

It seems like eons ago that I heard the first buzzzzzzzzzz of my electric razor. Not only had I grown older since then, but wiser too. I graduated from the safety of the electric model to a more skin-friendly model. Over the years I had run through the entire spectrum of shavers, trying almost every brand and model available. I nicked my way through the disposable, cringed through the straight edge, until finally finding a smooth ride with a razor made specifically for women. What a novel idea, a shaver designed for our unique contours, which astonishingly enough, manages to even glide over the ankle bones without slicing or dicing along the way.

In my younger days, shaving was a real drawn-out and time-consuming responsibility, one I took very seriously. First I'd shower, then dry. Next I'd move to the vanity, fill the sink and test the waters, and like the three bears, ensure the temperature was just right—not too hot, not too cold, but just right. Then I would hike my foot onto the countertop, splash it with water, spread it with shaving cream and then carefully cut the stubbles.

The older I got, the more precious my time; the more of a hassle shaving became. I searched for ways to shorten the process. When the depilatory products hit the market, I thought my prayers had been answered.

No shaving, no cuts, no nicks. Quick, painless and easy hair removal. The advertisements were music to my ears.

I rushed out, paid the handsome price for the miracle product, and ran home to test the claims. However, precaution was in order. I was careful to read and follow the instructions on the can of stuff potent enough to eat away the toughest of my hay-textured hair.

After assuring myself of survival, I applied the thick cream on my legs. A burning sensation signaled the substance had settled in to do its thing. Sitting on the side of the tub, inhaling the nostril-burning fumes while twiddling my thumbs I waited the required fifteen minutes for the miracle mixture to remove all the hair beneath the thick layer of goo. And sitting in that environment, minutes seemed like an eternity.

Although the cream worked, I found my shaving-frenzy speed much faster. I had, after all, perfected the quickest possible manner in which to rid my female body of all unwanted, unsightly hair. I quit the shaving creams altogether and combined showering, soaping, and shaving. Confined inside a shower, I am forced to reckon with the hassle of growing hair on a daily basis. Finding a safer and less tortuous instrument combined with a faster method helped ease the pain a little, but not much.

After many years, days, and hours spent shaving every little crevice on my legs and underarms, I am tired of the task. As much as I hate to utter the words, I must admit, mother is right. There is nothing glamorous about shaving!

First there are the underarms. For image sake these little boogers have to be shaved almost every day. Dare I skip a day and wear a sleeveless shirt, those little "tell-tale stubbles" would be publicly detected.

When it comes to shaving, however, it's not the underarms that are the pits; it's the legs. Those long, tedious limbs require shaving *skill* to prevent permanent scarring. This time-consuming chore is not well suited to an impatient person like me. I despise shaving my legs, and sometimes it literally shows.

I am a seasonal shaver. With shorts, bathing suits, and constantly exposed legs, summer puts a real damper on my social life and me. Shaving really cuts into my spare time. On the contrary, winter is wonderful. Protected and shielded with various layers of clothing, my leg hair is allowed to grow wild. I love it, except for the winter I worked for the judge.

An attorney and I were talking in the hallway when my ballpoint pen fell to the floor. At the same instant we both bent over to pick it up. There at leg level I noticed he was staring at my legs. I followed his gaze to see what his fascination was all about. There, sticking out of my midnight black pantyhose, were long, blonde leg hairs. I about died on the spot. My flushed complexion robbed me of what little dignity I had left at that moment. I learned my lesson that day. From then on, I swore off wearing pantyhose in the winter. Pants provide a hair hiding place.

Just a few years ago, shaving once or twice a week would eliminate the threat of razor burns from those passing too closely to my skin. I have noticed the older I am getting, the faster those little hairs seem to resurface. Hair growth is the only thing that increases with age. Metabolism, stamina, and energy levels seem to all decrease with age. And it's said the amount of required sleep dwindles as we age. Let's not forget my personal favorite—the pert, ninety-degree angle at which breasts are initially positioned seems to falter and fall with every passing year. Oh, and I forgot, memory declines as well!

These days it seems like fertilizer has been applied

and the sprouts have to be cut back daily. I gave up skipping a day on my underarms years ago. That is now a daily chore. Unless of course I move to Europe, where unshaven underarms are acceptable. On my first trip to France I was repulsed at the sight of women with underarm hair long enough to tie in a bun. Now I wish I could grow some buns besides those that follow me wherever I go.

In all honesty, I don't have it that bad. Besides having more fun, being a natural blonde has another, more important benefit. Blonde hair all the way around. So I don't have to deal with black stubbles so prominent against the backdrop of beige skin that they seem to glow in the dark, which is even worse when hair begins growing in places best suited for a man.

Shortly after I began taking hormones I noticed some new hairs sprouting on virgin territory. Immediately upon seeing the foreign fuzz, I ran for the telephone, desperately seeking an answer.

"Mom, have I always had hair on my upper lip?" I asked in a panic.

Had it always been there and I was now paranoid? Or had the HRT caused my subdued manly facial features to spring forth from hair follicles never before seen?

"Oh, yes, I used to shave your lip as a child," she giggled, obviously insensitive to my panic attack. I was in no mood for jokes. She should have detected the horror in my voice.

"Thanks, Mom! No, really," I pleaded for more honesty and less humor.

"It's the hormones. Wait awhile and your mustache will really take shape as it begins to thicken," her cruelty continued.

Joking or not, that was all I needed to hear. Panic really set in. I turned to another loving soul for reassurance. The moment he walked in the door I started quizzing my husband.

"Honey, have I always had this fuzz on my upper lip?" I nonchalantly asked of my adoring spouse as I bit that same lip which was now quivering in fear.

"Don't worry, Sweetie. I will loan you my razor and teach you the art of shaving facial hair," he said with a sheepish grin.

Oh, to have a family full of comedians was so overwhelming at times! I rubbed my lip and tried again for the ever-elusive truth. Seeing me rub my lip caused an immediate reaction from my husband.

"Don't do that!" he yelled. His abruptness caused me to jump. "Don't rub your lip. It will only make the hair grow faster!"

Oh, how funny they are, they all are. I can't imagine getting such pleasure at the expense of such a sore subject. Shame on them all! This would come back to haunt them.

I'd have to take this matter into my own hands. So over the next few weeks I waited, I watched, and I counted. I got so sick of the little mustache hairs haunting my every waking hour that, in frustration, I decided to put an end to it all. No, I did not commit suicide, but I did end the life of my bothersome fuzz. With tweezers in hand, I plucked every one of the little suckers from my upper lip, and from my life! One by one the follicles fell and with them came the end of that hairy-tale.

THIRTEEN

A Stroll Down Recovery Lane

Oh recovery. How educational! How challenging! How memorable! I was told recuperation would be a long process, but hearing it and living it are two entirely different things.

"In three to four weeks you will begin to feel better, and after six weeks you can resume all normal activity," my doctor laid out the timetable.

Feeling like myself again seemed light years away, a mere mirage in the desert of discomfort. It was such a long, long time from surgery back to status quo.

The first few days, relief came in the form of pain pills. Drugs helped ease the pain and discomfort, but I weaned myself from their assistance as quickly as my body and mind would allow, pushing my threshold for pain to the limits. Drugs were a necessary, numbing evil for a short time.

Recovery robbed me of my routine. As would be expected, my slumber suffered significantly. I was unable to "spoon" with my spouse. This, more than the pain, caused a long period of restless nights. Having been married less than two years, I longed for the warmth of my husband's body, the softness of his skin nestled against mine, and the emotional comfort that comes only with that snuggling type of slumber. I was unable to feel the security that comes from his masculine arms being wrapped tightly around my chest as we drift off to sleep. Absent was the familiar feel of his round stomach as it molded into the small of my lower back.

After awhile, his reluctance to hold me became alarming. Weeks after surgery he was still at arm's length, a distance made larger by our king-size bed. I understood his concern for my condition, but I was healing and longed for his boa constrictor grasp. Chalking it up to exhaustion, I let him have his space for a time. He was, after all, working all day and nursing me all night, all the while dodging the swath cut by my emotional machete-sharp monologues.

However, enough was enough. I needed his tender touch in order to sleep soundly. Finally I inquired as to the lack of our late-night latching. His response was, of course, full of concern.

"I'm afraid if I hold you or snuggle with you that I will hurt you," he explained. "But I will be right here beside you."

That wasn't enough to lull me into a deep sleep, but for now it would have to do, at least until the healing was a little further along.

Each new day of the lengthy recovery process did bring healing. By the second week, the fourteenth day, about three hundred and thirty-eight hours after the operation (but who is counting?). I realized I was starting to feel better. The onset of a sneeze no longer brought huge doses of anxiety, panic and intense pain, but merely a pillow-braced achoo and a healthy hurt.

Although relief was slow in coming, it was welcomed in each and every form. Whether it was the return of normal, regular bodily functions, normal sleep patterns, the physical ability to walk without assistance, or an entire day without a pain pill, each milestone was a cause for celebration. The minor, as well as the major, were deeply appreciated. Almost every facet of my life was affected in some way, from the obvious to the surprising. Nothing, and no one, was spared the repercussions of recovery. I learned, time and time again, and heard it over and over again—healing is a long process.

"It just doesn't happen over night or within a week or even within months. You have had major surgery and your body has been through an awful lot," my husband, my mother and my friends reminded me constantly. After a week they all began sounding like a broken record, and I was mighty tired of the tune, not to mention their tone.

I was a very impatient patient and tended to rush my recovery, experiencing constantly the difference between feeling and healing. Let me make this perfectly clear, how well one feels should not be confused with how well one is healing. Little things drummed this fact into my thick, hard head. Whenever the pain subsided, the "old" me surfaced immediately, eager to get back to the business of living, the normal way of doing things.

The first morning I arose pain-free was eight long days after surgery. Thanks to me and my thoughtlessness and impatience, that painless period was reduced to a fleeting moment. I was lying on the sofa, entertaining myself via the boob tube. My side was sore and stiff, so I thought a change of position was in order. Without thinking, I attempted to turn over onto my other side. Attempting that little trick ended my painless period. It was a reverting recovery reminder. I would settle for soreness any day.

Later that night I tested my limits once again. Laziness outweighed sanity as I reached (as in stretching) for a pen situated inside my nightstand. It seems as though most of my creative thoughts occur at night, in the dark, and always after settling into my comfy and cozy bed. This is a hassle when I was healthy, but even worse when physically restricted.

I freely admit that on this particular occasion I was too lazy to *roll* out of bed and do things the proper way. No, I compromised, and tried stretching and reaching. The search for the pen was abandoned and the thought I was trying to write down was lost to my thoughtlessness, and the ensuing shooting pains across my stomach. Another educational encounter, another lesson learned, one I would not soon forget.

During this period of recovery I also discovered the true meaning of the phrase roll out of bed. Yes, within one month this hysterectomy patient not only learned how to roll out of bed in the least painful way, but invented new and creative techniques to avoid agony.

For extremely tough times I discovered the highly unattractive and unladylike doggie-style of getting out of bed. This method involves hiking the legs up, rolling over Rover and then crawling out of bed on all fours. It is less painful and strenuous than just springing forth. However, there is one warning for anyone brave enough to attempt this feat. It should not be tried in the presence of another living soul, especially of the opposite sex. The sight of a woman maneuvering in a four-legged fashion is a thing best done in private.

On those occasions where I found myself stranded in the

middle of the huge mattress, I discovered a more conventional means to get my feet onto the floor. This rawhide technique when mastered, involves *rolling, rolling, rolling . . . move 'em out, rawhide!* I would simply roll over and over again until there was nothing but thin air separating me from the hard floor below. Then I would pray for my bearings before hitting the ground!

The last technique was discovered in time and out of sheer boredom, wanting to try something new. The old saying, variety is the spice of life now applied to ways of maneuvering off the mattress. With time I began to feel better, and three weeks after surgery I was pulling myself out of bed using the side seam of the mattress. I called this method the seamstress exit strategy. Soon afterwards, I discovered that without proper healing time, this particular movement, can cause piercing pain.

However, the recovery road is not just pain-paved. There are some positive points along the way. Healing brought real growth, in many ways.

Others had mentioned the itch that healing produces, but I had never endured the itch before the Big H. To my surprise, it only took a week after surgery for this irritation to begin. First it was subtle, little tingling sensations just below the belly button. Then it intensified. Quickly it graduated to a whopping itch that could be relieved only through actual scratching.

I never quite figured out whether the itch was from the emerging shaven hairs or the actual healing process. Maybe it was a combination. And it really didn't matter. Relief, in the form of a scratch around my incision and bare spots, was all that concerned me.

There is nothing more unattractive than me scratching my body, especially with both hands in a frantic free-for-all frenzy in the area south of the bellybutton. I made certain no one other than my pets, witnessed the disgusting clawing of the crotch area. Even they were probably disgusted at the sight, not to mention the sounds. The relief was accompanied by the ecstatic ooohhhhhs and aaaahhhhhhhhs as each fingernail slid gently over those stubble-ridden areas. The same places, which had once been a forest, were now reduced to a field of emerging seedlings in need of scratching stimulation, fingernail fertilizer. I was only engaging in behavior that my body craved.

The sights and sounds of relief signaled my indulgence in the disgusting deed. If anyone had seen me partaking in this pleasure, ridicule would certainly have resulted. The teasing would have been unbearable at best, especially from my spouse. I could hear the exchange.

"You look like an orangutan," he'd laugh.

"No, there are a few subtle differences between me and my primate counterparts. Monkeys scratch their bodies without regard to who is watching. Being conscious of the ladylike lessons that my dear mother drummed into my head as a child, teenager and an adult, I take pride in the fact that I am always very careful only to scratch in the privacy of our home! So deal with it or I may try it at one of your company socials."

The truth be known, it wouldn't have really mattered had my husband witnessed my animalistic behavior. Some things in life are just worth the taunting and this was just one of those thangs. Nothing was going to rob me of the pleasure derived from my ape-scrape.

Not only is the recovery road rocky and rough, it is oh-so confining. After merely a week of rest and relaxation, stir-craziness had set in. What was remaining of my sanity was sinking, quickly. I had to escape the confines of my infirmary. Reading, scratching and rolling were old hat. I was bored to tears. The highlight of my day was bouncing from sofa to love seat, and then from the love seat back to the sofa. I didn't actually bounce. It was more a shuffle.

Fearful of sofa sores I decided a change was in order. The time was right for something new and different—lawn chair lesions. So with the speed of a snail I meandered to the patio door and looked outside. The sun was shining, the afternoon breeze was soft, and lovely light blue clouds were floating gently overhead. I watched from the window like a caged animal. I had to venture out. I just had to.

An idea came to mind, an errand that was not too demanding and one that wouldn't cause too much scolding from family members. Oh the excitement! An outing, my first outing. But what should I wear? I debated whether to don more than my customary recovery rags consisting of one of my husband's tee shirts. Nah! Thought of something more confining clinching and clinging to my stomach convinced me that less was better. Besides, the neighbors had probably seen worse.

With the fashion decision out of the way, I was soon waddling out the front door and down the driveway to check the mail. It was slow going, as if I was wearing cinderblock shoes. But it didn't matter much. I was in the great outdoors.

Going down the driveway was a wonderful and invigorating trip. Reaching my destination was certainly a success, for I discovered two cards from friends, as well as our income tax refund check. Eureka! That was certainly worth the effort.

However, the thrill was short-lived. When I turned to face the return trip, my smile turned upside down into a big, frown. With those few circular steps from the southern mailbox to my northern abode, the joy turned to panic. There was one thing I hadn't considered beforehand.

Like the homeowners, our driveway is anything but normal. To say it has an incline is like saying Mount Everest has a slight slope. I believe the concrete corridor outside our home could be used to train Olympic downhill skiing hopefuls for competition. And at that moment, in my weak condition, it seemed long enough to be used for the giant slalom.

Matter of fact, our driveway had seen a few icy adventures. Several winters ago, a blue norther descended upon these parts, plummeting temperatures into the single digits. Along with the frigid air came a light, steady stream of rain, which, upon landing, quickly turned to a thick layer of ice. Not anticipating the winter wonderland, that evening my husband parked his car in the usual spot atop the peak. The next morning the biggest challenge of his workday was how to get to his car without busting his butt on the slippery driveway slope. I watched from the front window as my non-penguin of a partner carefully skated towards his car.

Once safely inside his car, another problem presented itself: getting down the driveway without wrecking the car. One glance at the neighbor's car wedged snugly against a fire hydrant down the street described the danger. And our starting gate was higher, the slope more severe. It didn't take much for the real action to begin. My husband simply turned the key, started the engine, shifted out of park, and immediately the tires were in motion.

I held my breath as the car began slipping and sliding sideways, gaining speed down the driveway, stopping only when it slammed into a curb across the street.

Except for my rapidly-pounding heart bruising my chest, no damage was done. He had maneuvered the ice-covered slope like a professional downhill skier, and with the excitement of a child.

"Man, that was fun! I wish I could do it again," he yelled as he slowly slid away to work.

It was only now, as I peered up the peak before me that the past performance of the Auto Icecapades came to mind. The huge slope was one small factor I hadn't considered until now, when it was much too late. Here I was way *down* yonder, at the bottom of the hill. The uphill climb staring down at me, daring me. My feet froze with fright.

I didn't have much choice. I had to get back to the house or call for help, and since I was clad only in my skivvies, that wasn't a very enticing proposition. I could hear my brother's favorite saying: If you're gonna be dumb, you gotta be tough.

Well, this recovery business had definitely taught me that. I was, maybe not dumb, but a little shy of smart when it comes to this healing stuff. And tough I was well on my way to becoming. With no viable options, my upward journey commenced. At least I was not alone; my dog was right beside me, lending moral support.

Halfway up the driveway I stopped and looked down at my constant and loyal companion. I wondered why she was there, walking so slowly in step with every feeble step I made. She couldn't catch me if I fell. Pity. I assumed it was pity that placed her there. I looked down at her and smiled.

"Angel, has this driveway always been this steep?" I questioned her.

The compassion in her saucer eyes, the affectionate wagging tail, revealed her purpose. Her presence and her loyalty said it all. "Mom, we will do this together."

The two of us managed the mountainous terrain, back

to the comforts of our home. It had been a difficult and drain-ing journey. Nevertheless, I had overcome the challenge and conquered the course. Once atop my destination, I was over-come with a sense of jubilation. Victory. Victory is all mine!

At that moment visions of how best to honor my accom-plishment flashed in my mind. There was always the tradition-al method of planting an American flag at the top of the peak. Or there was the more "religious" approach, a papal procedure. Physically able, I would have knelt and kissed the ground. However, I just opted to go back inside and assume my hori-zontal position on the sofa, where I was content to stay for the remainder of the afternoon.

The next day I peered from my window and watched as the mailman again placed something in our box. Not wanting to succumb to temptation, I convinced myself he had left nothing but bills. Now there really was nothing left for me to do but vegetate.

Along with boredom, guilt moved in and took up resi-dency at the three-week mile marker. There was so much to do and so little ability to do it. Oh, I had the time. Time is definitely what I had a lot of. It was muscles and strength which I lacked. At the halfway point of recovery, I was beginning to halluci-nate. Insanity had taken over. Even the prospect of undertak-ing the dreaded housework was becoming appealing. Besides that, the house was a wreck. New, was being confined to and forced to stay inside the wreck twenty-four hours a day, seven days a week.

I had nothing to do but stare at all that surrounded me, and it wasn't a pretty sight. Everywhere I looked there was dust. Up and down, and all around, layers of particles, dust balls and cobwebs were staring back at me, laughing now that their squatter's status graduated to full-time residents. A change prompted by the fact there was no longer anyone willing, or able, to displace them, combat their presence, and annihilate their very existence.

The more I stared the worse it got. The television screen had become a petri dish for growing the disgusting fuzz. My décor had somehow transformed from traditional to dust-deco, evident by the film-laden coffee table. The blades of the ceiling fan overhead wobbled from the weight of the buildup. The house was engulfed in a duvet of dust. Not an inch was spared the pesky particles. I was a sitting duck, a perfect target for death by dust inhalation.

But that wasn't all. The upheaval didn't end with dust. There were floors to be swept and mopped, carpets to vacuum, and furniture to polish. Everywhere I turned there was something to be done, a household chore calling my name, needing my attention. And there I was, lingering horizontal, doing the sofa samba. Doom had definitely descended. All the bouquets had all been delivered, died and been discarded. The phone calls ceased, and the mailman resumed his routine of bringing only bills.

For me, this halfway recovery point was the worst. It was then that all the well wishers had heard enough, plus learned the hard way not to ask a rather innocent question like How are you doing? It was then that my husband had done enough and had tired of all my requests, however small or tall. And it was then that I had sat on my butt enough. Enough was enough, and three weeks of convalescence was most definitely enough for me!

However, three weeks is, unfortunately, not enough. It was very difficult for me to admit that my body (and my doctor) could know better than MY mind. Yet, it took only two days of attempting to shake and bake myself into a Martha Stewart double for me to surrender to the requests of my body. "Are you nuts? We haven't finished healing yet, far from it," my insides mocked at me. "We have not adjusted to all this emptiness. This recent reconfiguration is still mending. Do you mind? "So I succumbed; regained my senses and resumed my lethargy.

Recovery is certainly a family matter, affecting every member of the household, and not just the two-legged members. I knew about their hardships (in no uncertain terms, they all let me know about it). But I was referring to the *children* of our clan. They were suffering, as well.

During the months prior to surgery, I had grown accustomed to walking our dogs down a nearby country lane paralleling a river. Regardless of my mood, nature always had a calming effect. It was magical how the outdoors always restored my peace and serenity.

Outdoor outings had become a ritual for us all. Merely the sight of me putting on tennis shoes sent the dogs running to the door, wagging tails signaling their excitement and eagerness to load-up. We would pile into our mutt mobile and off to our secluded spot we would go. Once we piled out, the fun began. Slowly I would walk along, taking in all the wonders of nature, watching the birds overhead and the gaggle of geese gathered in the fields nearby.

This setting was the pooches' playground. My big dog loves to hunt, or at least likes to think she can. The little one tries desperately to imitate her actions, not quite certain of the purpose of the chase. It doesn't take much for a parting of our ways, an unusual sight or sound always does the trick. And off they go. They love to chase rabbits or anything else that tests their hunting ability, speed, and endurance.

Their attempts are a real source of entertainment for me, good for a chuckle, or at the very least, a broad smile. The sight of Mutt and Jeff running (mostly in circles) in search of elusive wildlife is amusing. I always remain close, ready to lend moral support for the moment of truth when they come back empty-pawed.

Now those times were a mere memory of doggone yesterdays. Talk about life-altering surgery. This woman who once found joy and peace in a two-mile walk, twice a day, every day, was now reduced to a less strenuous form of exercise, like walking from the living room to the bedroom, to the bathroom.

This wasn't so earth-shattering to me. I could view this (and often did in the beginning) as a much welcomed vacation from exercise, a lazy sabbatical. But to the dogs, whose whole day revolves around our outings, not running for weeks was devastating, and produced a couple of pitiful pooches.

After surgery they truly led dogs' lives. The rowdy one was sent to grandma's for a visit. Once back home, both were banned from the bedroom. The sofa was off-limits. My stomach could no longer be used as a cushion for their comfort. Their hairbrushes lay still, and soon they learned to do the same.

The daily routine of our pampered pooches was altered, and life as they knew it halted. They were reduced to spending most of their day lying quietly on the floor beneath the sofa where I lounged. After a week or two, sad and despondent expressions appeared on their mugs. They knew I was hurting, but it was apparent they were also in agony. They too had undergone a traumatic change in life—the loss of their lengthy, daily romp in the woods.

For the first two weeks of recuperation, their *dad* had exercise detail. It was not quite as lengthy or adventuresome, but as long as they were unleashed and on a free spree, it was okay by them, at least for the first few weeks. Being the spoiled brats they are, they wanted it back the way it was, with mom in the driver's seat.

Soon their wish was granted. At the three-week point I received my driving papers. I was about to encounter freedom, life without confinement. In need of a whole lot of serenity, it was not surprising that my first escapade behind the wheel involved a wilderness walk with my kids. After all they had been so good and understanding of our situation.

Once I managed to maneuver myself behind the wheel, I discovered there was a difference between being medically released to drive and physically fit to drive. However, we managed to make it to our tranquil spot without running off the road, crashing into a tree or broadsiding a barn.

The tires hadn't come to a full and complete stop (only a slight slow down), when the overly excited, eager-beaver canines jumped from the truck hellbent on running free. The only thing I saw was the backsides of a small and a large animal scattering into the wild blue yonder. But wait! Something was awry. My constant companions soon realized something was missing; namely *their* companion. Suddenly both put on the brakes and came to an abrupt halt. They then turned inquisitively towards the truck, noticing I had never strayed from my pilot position in the cab of the truck.

What? Mommy is not walking in the woods with us? they seemed to mutter. Whoa. Wait a minute. Not only that, she's getting away!

They ran, fast and furious, back toward the truck and watched in bewilderment as I slowly drove forward. Outside of the driver's side door they stood, waiting and watching as

I inched the vehicle a little way down the road.

"Come on, walk," I instructed out the window as I puttered forward. But they didn't follow. Frozen in their paw-steps, they stood still cocking their head from side to side in pure puzzlement. This activity was not only strange; it defied all logic. They had been taught never to chase a vehicle, even being scolded for merely thinking about it. Now their mom was coaxing and commanding them to follow a moving truck. Go figure!

Crawling at a speed of less than five miles per hour, I watched them carefully in my side mirror, waiting for them to follow my lead. Finally I had gotten too far away from them for comfort. Their bewilderment turned to panic as the distance between them and the truck widened. Scared of being left behind, they set their paws in motion until they caught up to the truck. There alongside the truck, they vowed never to let me get away, never to leave their sight.

It took several minutes and a whole bunch of pleading before they caught on to the new trick. Soon they were leisurely walking beside the truck as I slowly drove on down our road. Once they got used to my strange new method of walking them, they were a little less apprehensive. They even became comfortable enough to venture out to the woods . . . for very brief moments. The thought of being left behind, without a ride home, usually kept them close by.

None of us were ever comfortable with this new form of exercise, but after awhile, we all came to understand that desperate times call for desperate measures. It would just have to do until the recovery was complete and life and normalcy returned. If ever it did exist.

At least I was driving again. That was surely a peddle in the right direction. But looming ahead was yet another detour on the rough and rocky recovery road. Physically I was healing fine, but mentally I was deteriorating. By the fifth week things had taken a turn for the worse. Frustration, impatience, and boredom took over mind, body, and soul. Gone was the grin-and-bear-it, happy-go-lucky girl that once resided in our home. No doubt about it, thirty-five days of being a slug transformed this lady of the house into a monster of the moors.

This period was, by far, the most painful. I was miserable, my stomach was sore to the touch, and I had aches and pains in places never before known to me, all of which prompted another round of moans and unending groans. My bitching caused those around me to be sick and tired, too. It was a vicious cycle.

I didn't understand this point in my physical pilgrimage. And I wanted to know why. NO! I demanded to know what was causing my added aches so far along in recovery. Why was my healing headed backward instead of forward? My husband tried desperately to console me and calm me, before I did something drastic.

"You have had major, major surgery," he said.

No kidding. Now tell me something I don't already know, I wanted to snap back but bit my tongue instead.

"Have you ever broken a bone?" he inquired sweetly.

` "No," I answered promptly and proudly, as I knocked on wood—just for good measures.

"Well, I have, and remember the more I healed, the more it hurt."

I stared at him with a dumb blonde look, "Huh?"

My dear husband then proceeded to explain his theory of muscle aches. His rationale was simple. The more I healed, the more I moved dormant muscles, the sorer they became.

"You said your stomach hurt when you lifted your leg? Well, it was the first time since the surgery that you have done that so it is bound to cause some soreness," he assured me. "You are using muscles you haven't used recently."

I am sure he was hoping my jaws muscles would take a rest as well. Okay that all made a little bit of sense. I now had a choice. Continue to stretch the limits, invoke the pain, or continue vegetating.

Mind over matter. I would not voluntarily become a couch potato. I decided to push the limits and press the lips shut. Eventually I adjusted my thinking, learning to sit back and enjoy the ride, squeezing those lemons into lemonade. My attitude adjusted, changing from one of a

prisoner waiting to be freed to that of a princess in waiting. Soon my carriage would arrive to carry me back to
normalcy . . . or to the nut house.

FOURTEEN

Weighing
the Facts

Rumor has it that undergoing the Big H not only makes some women better, but also bigger. Some physicians disagree, saying it depends on the patient. Then what do they know? I wonder how many of them can personally testify to the facts.

As vain as it may sound, one of my main concerns about the operation was not the medical risk during, but the weight gain afterwards. Considering my cellulite-centered obsession this fear was well-founded. During my initial discussion with my surgeon, I wasted no time in sorting facts from fiction, cutting through all the bull and getting down to the bare essential, important stuff.

"Tell me about the weight gain associated with a hysterectomy. I want the truth as you have personally witnessed-with your postoperative patients. No holds barred. I want the whole scoop on this subject, Doc. So please don't sugarcoat it. Just give it to me straight."

Again, I must reiterate the fact that my surgeon is a man—a mere male mortal, incapable of fully understanding the female mentality. His answer further proved this point.

"Oh, that is really nothing to worry about," he tried to calm at least one of my fears quickly shifting the topic from the scales back to the scalpel.

Now that I have been there and done that in regards to this surgery, I'm an expert of sorts on this touchy topic of postoperative poundage attributable to surgical menopause. I feel as a red-blooded, American, wombless woman it is my duty to inform women worldwide of the true correlation between losing a uterus and gaining weight. Therefore, I will reveal the real skinny on my weight before, during, and after surgery. This means one thing, the need to divulge my bulge, that top-secret, highly confidential material. Only for womanhood would I consider breaching such highly sensitive, top-secret (as well as unpleasant and degrading) information.

If I was going to be the guinea pig for the research, I was going to make certain everything was done properly. Research needed to be done. Precise data had to be collected. This, of course, meant only one thing. I was having to step where I vowed to never step again. It was back to the scary scales. But what the heck, it was for a good cause.

Before undergoing the knife, it registered 110 pounds, and I (accurately) recorded this number under lock and key. To honestly report the effects of surgery I must first admit to my defects. Preop there was a small (relatively speaking) tummy pooch situated just below my bellybutton, right above the biki-ni line. I thought it was kinda cute and chalked it up to gravi-ty. However, postoperatively it was a different story altogether.

Once home from the hospital that little pooch had mul-tiplied into plural pooches. The operation had definitely taken its toll on my tummy, causing a ripple effect around my waist-line. Now there was not one, not two, but three budding bulges. One was disgusting enough, but three were a horrifying sight to this vain dame.

Swelling, it has to be just the swelling! That's gotta be it! I cried and cringed at the sight before me. I crossed my fingers and hoped as time passed the swelling would subside and the emerg-ing abdominal hills and valleys would erode into flatlands.

Thinking they were only temporary reminders of the surgerical recuperation still underway, I initially dismissed the little pouches above and below my bellybutton. However, time gave way to intelligence. Those bulges became a constant companion encompassing my waist, turning my hourglass shape into a borderless bowl.

My stomach (all three of them) looked horrible. It was too much for me to bare, or bear. So much so that I reverted to sleeping in pajamas. I did not want my husband seeing or feel-ing my tummy. It was off-limits, therefore so was hugging or snuggling or any other action that would require physical con-tact with my stomach. I dressed in the closet and undressed in the bathroom, out of sight of husband and mirrors. I was worse than a vampire steering clear of reflective glass images.

During this traumatic time I also dodged the scales. Ignorance in this particular situation truly was bliss. Not knowing exactly how much weight I had gained improved my outlook as well as my sour-grape disposition. I just bitched about my bulges day and night to everyone that had ears and would listen. Soon my husband grew tired of all my complaining.

"You don't even know how much weight you have actually gained, and you won't until you get on those scales. Instead of griping all the time, why don't you just go in there, get on the scales and see if it is really as bad as you imagine?"

But did I really want to know those ghastly fat facts? Did I really want to know exactly where I stood on the great scales of life? Did it matter? Would it make a difference? Would knowing relieve the situation, or lessen the problem? I think not!

However, as pressure built inside the home, I caved in. Curiosity had gotten the best of me. Finally, two weeks after surgery, I mustered the nerve to get my head out of the sand and my feet onto the scale.

Our scale is conveniently hidden in the master bathroom, in the farthest corner, against a wall, behind the toilet. Out of sight, out of mind was my rationale. And this scale was not just any old scale. Nope, nothing ordinary about it. In our house our scale is the most technologically advanced weight-measuring apparatus money could buy. Accuracy is of the utmost importance when it comes to an instrument that determines my mood in a matter of seconds, in a matter of numbers.

This new and improved, modern bathroom scale was a recent purchase, one of those things I just had to have. Not only does this scale give a very *large*, leave-nothing-to-question, bright red digital readout of your weight, but it also delivers a double whammy. Another disgusting piece of information is also included during the monumental moment of truth. A second large, bright red digital reading is also revealed: the percentage of body fat. Even worse then the information is the fact that I paid good money for this all-too-honest, acutely accurate, demeanor-damaging instrument! Talk about self-inflicted wounds.

At very rare times I found this scale to be a real treasure. After surgery was one such occasion, as those digital digits read three pounds less than before the operation. I couldn't believe my eyes or the number registering underneath my feet! An amazing three pounds had been shed somewhere along the way. I wondered how much a uterus weighed.

Of course, my weight loss could have been due to the recent lack of appetite. I hadn't felt much like eating since surgery. When I don't feel good, I don't eat. I ate only what was necessary to keep on the good side of those watchful do-gooders. My husband and mother constantly quizzed me on my food intake and then analyzed the nutritional value of it all.

Whatever the reason, the weight loss was certainly an extra bonus to undergoing the Big H and the first postoperative positive encountered. The good news really lifted my spirits. I was beginning to think the excess baggage surrounding my waist had somehow drifted downward and had become a permanent fixture on my thighs. But now it was coming off. Oh, how sweet it was. And oh, how short-lived.

Only a few weeks later my appetite for life resumed. The incredible shrinking thighs soon gave way to an expand-o-rama phenomenon, which engulfed not only my waist and thighs, but my buttocks as well.

This cellulite surge I felt was only natural. After all, there is no way a woman can be inactive for days, weeks and months and not gain a few extra pounds, I reasoned. Unless, of course, I refrained from eating entirely. Starving myself was the last thing I wanted to do. On the contrary, I viewed recovery as a perfect excuse to get horizontal and eat bonbons. So I indulged and pampered myself, though I knew better. My metabolism did not come to life with that first slap from the obstetrician way back when. As I emerged from the birth canal, my metabolism escaped. And its been on the run every since. I gain weight from merely glancing at sweets. Weight always weighs heavy on my mind.

Now I had a good excuse to indulge in life. After all, I was recovering from *major* surgery. So I pigged out and ate what I dared not eat before: ice cream, candy, and junk food, all those forbidden fruits. I actually went bonkers and asked my husband to buy a half-gallon of cellulite-enhancer, more commonly known as ice cream. Over a three-day period, I shoveled spoonfuls of the delightful, fattening luxury into my mouth without forethought or fear. I was on autopilot, in ice-cream overdrive, and my destination was "Thighland."

Not surprisingly, it all took its toll and began to show. Before I knew it my saddlebags were back—and full to their brims, overflowing with fatty tissue and cellulite. It seemed as if I had ballooned overnight. However, the full extent of my indulgence did not become apparent until four months later when my husband bullied me back onto the scales. With that one step began yet another battle of the bulge.

I had fought this battle most of my life, engaging in constant caloric combat from puberty on. I had run the gamut from a shrinking kid to an incredible bulk as my figure fanned from skinny peaks to broad valleys. My closet contained clothes of every size, from 2 to 12, and at one time or another I had worn them all. I have stretch marks on my chest and thighs, not from childbearing but from weight bearing! My lifelong struggle against the persistent pound consisted of weighing, wavering, and always worrying.

However, I have an excuse. At a height of five feet one and a half inches (that half inch counts for a lot, too), I am not fat, just short. With that build, things are certainly stacked against me. Every ounce gained seems to result in a roll, or two.

I did have one skinny stint. During the bleakest time in my life, motivated by utter despair and depression, I shrank to a record ninety-five pounds. While some women may long for such a weight, this was not only the darkest of my days but by far the worst I ever looked. I was ashamed and frightened at the reflection, which greeted me each morning—the skin and bones, the outline of every rib so vivid in the mirror before me. My biggest fear quickly turned from being too fat to being too thin. I tried to hide my hideous shell from my mother, for I knew if she saw my haunting figure it would crush her

Needless to say I did not stay at that weight. Anything that caused me to hide in shame was not something I aspired to remain. Being grotesquely underweight was not attractive to me and thin was well, under-rated in my opinion. As far as I was concerned, being a scarecrow was for the birds. And it was a good thing, too. Once my troubles ended, I had no problems putting the pounds back on.

When my husband first laid eyes on me I was at an ideal weight. This of course was not the result of dieting, determination, or dedication. Nope, my willpower was, is and will probably always remain powerless over food. I was a slim and trim petite person only because of my workaholic lifestyle. My life consisted of burying myself in work, on the run ten to sixteen hours a day, six days per week. I thrived on the adrenaline rushes that come with a reporter's job, the endless emergency calls, and ensuing assignments and stories. And there was little time for merriment, meals, or munching of any sorts.

I was always on the move and liked it that way. Having had my fill of failed relationships, I figured it was the safest way to travel—a moving target is harder to hit. Obviously, my husband blew a hole into that theory of mine. If I may say so, I didn't look too shabby on our wedding day, wearing my size 2, stylish lace wedding dress. That glorious day ended my reign as an ever-evasive moving target, as well as causing a temporary ceasefire in the battle of the bulge. Marriage is the most fattening thing I've ever encountered.

Not only did I become plump and personable with marriage, so did my other half. In only a few short years his college physique gave way to a spare tire, and a semi-tractor trailer tire at that. We had settled down, settled in, and it all settled on us in unsightly ways, in all-too apparent areas.

However, there were big differences between my weight gain and his, besides the numbers. Mine was a source of contention, as he dropped not-so-subtle reminders of how much weight I had gained since we married. My gains were obviously his loss. His weight, on the other hand, is a sensitive issue, completely off conversational limits. It didn't matter that I had gained only a meager molehill compared to his massive mountain. Therefore, the few pounds I lost after surgery were a welcome relief, however short-lived.

It didn't take long for that little lost weight to find its way back home. Sitting around all day bored to tears with nothing to do and no one to do it with left a person little to do but munch the day away. When I felt sorry for myself, I cheered me up with a treat, usually of the fattening sort. I never sang the blues without being accompanied by a quartet of soda pop, chips, dips, and nuts. When I had a recovery benchmark to celebrate, I did it with a delicacy. When I needed to be pampered, the cupboard came calling. It didn't matter that I was the only one that attended my pity parties. That just meant all the junk food was mine. I had stocked the cabinet well, and it was showing on my emerging thunder thighs. Unfortunately, those lost pounds compounded before becoming reunited with my body.

After only a few weeks of self-indulgence, I was bulkier than before. The worst part of my bulging body was the clothing aspect. My current wardrobe no longer fit. I was forced to reach for my fat clothes, that womanly line of clothing hidden in the corners of the upstairs closet, which until now had been out of sight and out of mind. Once I located the dusty mothball-scented wardrobe and removed it from its hiding place, I tried on the ancient apparel. I was shocked at the results.

"My gosh! Even these gargantuan garments don't fit," I disgustingly screamed at myself.

They were all too little, too tight for my now well-rounded, around-and-around, figure. Embarrassed by my weight gain, I hated to venture outside. Home was my sanctuary, a shield against all the comments and stares, which were surely awaiting me.

To say I was depressed or upset would have been a real understatement. I couldn't figure how all this happened so quickly. I knew why it happened but it came on so fast and with such magnitude. I know my body and I certainly know my weight gain patterns, but this was not normal. Whatever the reason, the result was the problem. Pigging out had a price—and I was paying.

So on with the battle and off with the bulges. I was committed to walking away the weight. Even before I was completely healed I started walking three miles a day, every day. I pushed myself in an attempt to shed the pounds. I would walk, week after week, and then weigh, convinced that some of that unsightly cellulite was left along my route. Wrong! Always wrong, always the same digital number on the scales.

How could this be? I cut back on food, increased my water intake, ate apples, oh, so many apples, and nada! That same stupid number always beamed back at me.

I was so good, even deleting snacks of every shape and size from my diet completely. Seldom would I crave a snack, but on those rare occasions I'd indulge only in pretzels, then only ten, and unlike me they were the fat-free variety. I became label conscious and serving wise. I knew there were only one hundred calories and zero fat content in that size serving of pretzels.

I took pride in my dedication and endless effort. However, the more I tried, the tighter my clothes, and the more constricting the waistbands. I had outgrown my fatly fashions and now nothing fit my chubby, stubby shape.

I was determined not to buy any more rotund regalia. In desperation, I resorted to my other clothing line, the buried-beneath batch. These unsightly, way-out-dated clothes were under all the crap stored in the crevices of the closets. I went on another dig, in search of anything that would fit.

It was all so confusing to me. The scales registered eight pounds less than my pinnacle poundage, yet I could not fit into clothes that once hid my body at my poundage peak. Something was definitely wrong with this picture. My hips were the culprit, a barrier to all styles and sizes.

Then it occurred to me. The hormones, it had to be the hormones. When I was younger and waging a war against endometriosis, my gynecologist prescribed birth control pills to control the growth of the lining. I quickly blossomed into a bulging beauty back then, too. When I got tired of carrying an even heavier burden, I dispensed with the little, pink, rotating pill dispenser and swore I'd never subject myself to heavyweight hormonal remedies again.

Year after year, laser surgery after laser surgery, gynecologist after gynecologist, birth control pills came highly recommended as a way to curb endometriosis. I always refused, for the enemy in my eyes was not the pain associated with the growth threatening my internal organs, but the weight that would certainly appear—and adhere—to my petite external frame.

Now years later I was right back where I started, partaking of hormone pills. Again, those tiny tablets were causing me to bud, blossom, and bloom. That had to be it!

The topic of my weight gain began to consume me, and my conversations. I admitted my weight gain to all that would listen, for surely they saw. It soon became an obsession consuming even my cyberspace correspondence. My girlfriends, hundreds of miles away, were kept abreast as to my caloric crusade. Across the computer the e-mails detailed my dilemma.

"Hey girlfriend! Well, for entertainment last night I cleaned house. When I really wanted to have some fun, I tried on my fat clothes. I cannot believe it, but none of my fat clothes fit over my fat ass! Not one pair of jeans or slacks. I don't know what happened or how it happened so fat-fast, I mean. All right, I do know what happened; FAT jumped on my hips for a free ride. But how did that happen so quickly? Okay I am over it now. Today will be a better day. I am off to buy fat clothes. I wonder if I should go to a maternity shop where I know they will have clothes that will fit over my protruding stomach and bulging thighs. I hate going outside or anywhere that I can't wear one of my husband's extra-large tee shirts. We leave for Denver tomorrow. I can see and hear it now. We get pulled over for speeding. Sir, did you know you were traveling at 80 mph in a 75 mph zone? The officer interrogates my spouse. Who is that in the passenger seat and why is she naked? Oh that's my wife. She's gained so much weight that the only thing that fits her is what she has on now—her birthday suit.

Funny it was not. I swore the last time the unwanted and unsightly saddlebags disappeared it would be the last time. But I was wrong. Once again I was facing the tumultuous and tenacious trek of peeling of the persistent poundage. Under normal circumstances, that in itself is a frightening feat. But now I was under pressure. I had to prepare for an upcoming trip with my husband.

As much as I love to travel, this should have been a happy occasion. Wrong! Once pulled from the top of the closet, the dusty suitcases caused fear, panic, and sheer desperation. I had nothing to pack.

Bearing the Big H

It wasn't that I didn't know what proper attire to pack. Nope. It was far worse than ignorance. There were no clothes, suitable or otherwise, that would fit over my protruding thighs. If only my wardrobe had consisted of one size fits all instead of encompassing the entire sizing spectrum.

Regardless of my reluctance, I had to go shopping for something to wear on our upcoming trip. I had no choice. There was not enough time to drop the necessary pounds, or heal from liposuction.

So off to the store we went, my mother and I, in search of a few new items of clothing that would hide my body, or at least cover it. I was shopping spoiled and patronizing was not what it used to be. I went from living in a metropolitan city, the fashion Mecca of the south, to a town where a chain super store was the primary purveyor of clothing. Still, I tried my best under the circumstances, to find articles that would just get me by until we arrived in Denver, where I could shop until I dropped. Oh, how I looked forward to the stylish stores and big city lights.

I did manage to find one suitable women's clothing store in town. This shopping excursion was by no means fun, but rather a necessity, even more adequately described as nothing short of a desperate measure. And why I chose to take my mother, I will never know. It was certainly not for moral support.

Once inside a dressing room with a few articles of clothing, my mother was summoned for her critical eye and honest, sharp point of view. The first outfit included a denim skirt. I tried it on. Over my thunder thighs, up and over my hefty hips it slid, barely. So far so good. Oh, wait! There were the buttons still to be buttoned. I anxiously looked upward and prayed for some relief.

I pulled. I tugged. I paused and then pulled some more. The skirt seemed to be just an inch "short of material." How could that be? Maybe I grabbed an extra small, or even a small. It was bad enough that my normal size had to be abandoned in favor of the next size up. I reluctantly conceded to that fact. But please, dear Lord, don't make me go any further *up* that humiliating size chart.

A wave of nausea overcame me as I grabbed the tag and peered at the size. It was then that I heard the noise. A giggle, of all things, sounded behind me. What could possibly be fitting for humor in this dressing room scene? Where was that coming from? Better yet, who was doing it and what were they laughing about? Surely it was not my mother, for she knew how much this issue weighed on me, and how depressed and sick I was about the sudden outward shift in my figure.

I scanned the mirror before me searching for the culprit who dared to snicker. But only my mother's face reflected back. It was then that I knew.

"Mom, what are you laughing at?" the irritation and anger welled up inside me. "You know how upset I am over this! How could you possibly find anything amusing in this sickening scene?"

"I am sorry," she said over her giggles. "It was just the desperation on your face as you looked at the size tag."

That was all of that! Abruptly the new clothes were peeled off, and dropped to the floor. I put my muumuu back on and headed for the exit. Clothes or no clothes, I ended my search for anything that could camouflage and cover my new chubby *cheeks*. With time dwindling down, I would now be forced to pack my suitcase full of muumuus and one-sizers. So much for me being a walking fashion statement. What the heck? It was only a superficial shift. Internally I was the same. Beef or bones that would never change, I consoled myself.

However, I was still perplexed about the extent and distribution of my weight. Only one person knew the exact tally of the scales. Unfortunately, I had confided in my mother. But she too was as perplexed about my additional proportions. There was no explanation for the extra inches even with my binging. It just didn't add up.

As we drove home from the store, mom made a proclamation. I never knew if she made it to make amends, ease my poundage pain, or because she felt it was a plausible excuse.

"I've got it. I know why you have gained weight so

rapidly and for no good reason," she said. "It is the hormones. It has to be."

Great! She was on my side and verifying the medical malady which I was hanging my humiliation on. But short-lived it was, for my mother was not finished. No, her comforting excuse disappeared as she continued on with a conversation she had many years before with her gynecologist.

"Before my hysterectomy, I asked my doctor about weight gain, and if it would present a problem down the road," she relayed. Her doctor gave her a nonsense type of answer, one that unfortunately put the ball back in the patient's court.

"If you want to use this surgery as an excuse to gain weight, you will gain weight; however, if you don't want to gain weight, there is no medical reason you should."

Wonderful! I would now have my mother to contend with, reminding me of her doctor's opinion and her lack of weight gain, whenever I tried to correlate (blame) my weight gain on the hysterectomy.

Still I searched for answers, or maybe it was consoling and understanding I was really in need of. I consulted other postoperative patients. Sure enough, others admitted to gaining unwanted weight after the Big H. They too, felt the tilt of the scale happen after partaking in the *harmony* pills. Not only that, but after further hysterectomy harping with my cohorts, I learned my hormone dosage was twice their dosage. No wonder there was a rise in my thighs. This was glorious news. I had twice the excuse of any woman I knew. But I had to know if this hormone theory was correct. Immediately my gynecologist was consulted, via the quickest possible route, an emergency e-mail was sent into cyberspace.

"Hi Doc! Now help me! Does the hormone you prescribed for me cause weight gain? This is serious and not a time for humor. So don't be funny, just answer the question, please. Hurry!"

Tapping my fingers on the desk, I patiently waited for an answer. But that familiar "you've got mail" queue never came. So another, more urgent, high priority message was sent.

"Hi there. I just wanted you to know that when I sent the

SOS message earlier about the weight, I was on top of a building standing on the ledge waiting for an answer, the right answer. Since I did not receive a reply in a timely fashion I have decided to jump. No, you're not in my will. I just wanted you to live with the guilt."

Signing off the computer I sat at my desk and looked at the ground below me. Okay so I exaggerated a little. Still it wasn't worth it I decided. A jump from the second story of our home would only cause me more pain.

FIFTEEN

Trippin' Out

The business trip had been planned for months, long before surgery was even contemplated. My husband and I had previously planned on making the most out of it by piggybacking our vacation on his business trip. I will never understand the ways of the business world. Board of directors get together, decide to spend time in the Rocky Mountains, and then have the audacity to call it a *business* trip. But I can't complain. So happens my husband sits on that board. And being a dedicated person, he feels it's his duty to always attend such gatherings, especially when they're held somewhere exciting. Besides, this was a perfect opportunity to escape the stagnant, stifling summer heat.

There was only one small problem, namely me. The closer the departure, the more my husband was overcome with spousal concern. He feared I was not physically fit for a five-day driving vacation through the mountainous terrain of the Rockies. I wondered if he was more concerned with wasting his precious vacation time than with my recuperation. There was no end to his monotonous monologue.

"I don't think you are really up to this Honey, and we shouldn't do anything that would interfere with your recovery" he rationalized. "You know how you are. You're going to get depressed when you're unable do things that you want to do. We will be back in Denver in a few months, and can take a few extra days then. Let's wait on our vacation."

Oh, he is such a sensible soul—an engineer to the core. What else can I say? I, on the other hand, am very irrational, especially where travel is concerned. I would never let a little surgery and pain get in the way of traveling. I was not only born to shop but also born to boogey. Besides, a diversion was in order. Driving through the Rocky Mountains would get my mind off my aches and pains. The beauty of the snow-capped mountains and smell of spruce trees would certainly do the trick. Oh, I knew it would be just what the doctor ordered. I saw it as a small spoonful of sugar to help the healing process go down.

Wrong, wrong, wrong! We drove the nine hours to Denver without much fanfare other than being cramped inside a car as we crossed very dry and dull scenery. But all in all it was going well. I took a pillow along, which was not unusual. Only this time the pillow was not only intended to support my hard head but also my tender tummy. The feather-filled shock absorber was pressed snugly against my abdomen every mile of the way. It did the trick, for my internal organs did not spring forth from my stomach during the entire journey.

Being confined in a car, nowhere to run, no way to escape for hours upon hours, our road trips are sometimes a source of marital mayhem. I believe the corresponding legal term is entrapment. With limited means of entertainment, I usually try my hand at an old-fashioned pastime called conversation, the true two-way dialogue type conversation. Not the usual marriage monologue where the wife speaks and an occasional nod is seen or an indifferent grunt is heard from the husband as he continues reading his newspaper or watching the television.

The car is cause for an attentive, captive audience. And believe me, I always take full advantage of this type of situation. Given my recent fatty fashion fiasco, there was only one conversational topic to indulge in: the heavy stuff. I wasted no time in pouncing my vehicular victim.

"Honey do you think I am still as attractive as when we married?" Oh what a loaded question!

"Yes Darling. Why do you ask?"

Oh, don't give me that crap! Anyone who is not legally blind can figure out why I am asking, I thought to myself.

"Well, fortunately, I can't see my backside, my butt to be exact, and I was just wondering if I had gained so much weight there that you no longer find me attractive. I can't believe I could ever let myself go like this."

This called for a very diplomatic response and one any

fool would consider carefully before speaking. I could see the wheels turning in my husband's head as he weighed each word very cautiously before uttering a single syllable.

"I can see that you have gained a little weight since your surgery but it is not that much."

Oh what a sweet (or blind) man I had married.

"Yeah, but the scales do not justify the actual inches that have formed around my torso and thighs," I explained, still seeking a sympathetic response.

Desperate for affirmation and approval, I proceeded to rationalize my weight gain, detailing my theory correlating hormones and the ensuing weight gain.

"This just has to be the answer because it happened before when I was on the pill," my rationalizing went on. "This is just history repeating itself."

To say his response caught me off guard would be an understatement. It downright knocked me out of my passenger seat.

"Well, Honey, if I had a choice between you being hefty or grouchy, I would choose hefty," he said without a hint of a smile, without any trace of humor. I think he was serious!

I was shocked into silence. I couldn't believe my ears. My husband had, in one sentence, summed up his opinion of two very sensitive subjects: my newly acquired full-figure and my recent emotional state. Now the truth was out. There was no taking it back. He had bluntly spilled his guts with two words that cut me to the quick. He called me hefty—a word I was certain had been derived from the word heifer, a cow no less. To add insult to injury, he obviously was insinuating I had not been such a loving and sweet wife lately. I guess grouchy is somewhat better than being described as bitchy. Wow! Who was the fool that said honesty is the best policy? From then on the golden of silence escorted us to the Mile High City.

I would never admit it to my other half, but the drive knocked the wind out of my sails, taking its toll on my recovery, both physically—and now emotionally. So, I spent the next several days in the hotel room, in my usual horizontal position, watching television and ordering room service. For the most part things were great. A change of indoor scenery brought about a real attitude adjustment. I was content just laying around and looking out onto the hustle and bustle in the streets of a major metropolitan city spread out below our hotel window. It was entertaining, in a confining sort of way.

After a few days, however, things took a turn for the worse. There I was doing what I do best, lying in bed watching television, when I noticed something very odd. I was straining to peer over, and past, what resembled a potbelly. My stomach had grown, not just a little, but a lot. It was protruding in a most unsightly manner.

Immediately I knew something was wrong. My food intake had not changed, nor had my outtake. But there before my very eyes was this hot air balloon ready for launching. I was afraid that if anything touched the inflated tummy, it would burst, propelling me into the air, twisting and twirling toward the upper atmosphere at the speed of sound.

I lay there and looked. Puzzled and panicked. Then I wondered and I worried. My stomach had been swollen since surgery. But this was fatter and farther than before. That evening the increased size of my tummy was the topic of the dinner discussion between my husband and me. We could only guess the cause. Later, I discovered that other hollowed heroines had also experienced this freakish phenomenon. It seems altitude affects more than just breathing. It sometimes brings about some serious bloating, which I am happy to report deflates upon descent.

The end of the business meeting brought about the end of my leisurely lounging days and the beginning of our quality time. We were set to venture into the mountains, in search of rest and relaxation. And we had five full days in which to find it.

We wasted no time in making tracks. Packing, checking out, and hitting the road were all completed in record time. Through Rocky Mountain National Park to Grand Lake, to Vail and Maroon Bells, over Independence Pass, and up Pike's Peak we traveled. All day long, for six to eight hours per day, for five long days we traveled, and traveled, and traveled some more, all in a rental car. They refer to it as a mid-size. Yeah right. The more we traveled, the more I felt like a sardine trapped inside a tin can, a very flimsy, lightweight tin can.

There is nothing mainstream about our traveling style. We are off the beaten path type vacationers, preferring to travel the more scenic, less congested, country roadways instead of interstates and highways. Only this time, this trip, the winding, mountainous roads resembled washboards.

The vacation designed to take my mind off my tummy did just the opposite as every jiggle jolted me back to reality. At times I began to wonder if shock absorbers were extra on rental cars, available only with an upgrade.

For days we drove the back roads—the rough, rocky, dirt roads—that did nothing more than drive home the fact that I had not fully healed. I worried that this adventure was undoing all the healing I had done. The terror of the terrain took its toll. And my limitations brought on lamentations. And torture...

I love to raft and hike with my husband every chance we get. And we never missed an opportunity to indulge in the thrills of nature's playground. But this trip was the exception, a fact that was rubbed in my face at every turn of our travels. Everywhere we went there was white-water rafting, the adventurous, exhilarating kind—my most favorite kind.

Time to time we would stop the car and watch as the thrill-seekers sailed by on the roaring river. First I would moan and groan about my bystander status. Then pouting would quickly follow. I wanted so badly to get in a raft and venture downstream. I was not stupid though. I didn't even ask, although the constant whimpering sounds that came from my sealed lips did manage to let my husband know beyond a shadow of a doubt what my heart longed for: white-water rafting.

To me there was nothing more musical than the gurgling sounds of a wild, mountain snowmelt river as it roars over the rocks, signaling its passage down the winding riverbed. Unable to raft in it, we decided to picnic beside it.

I had packed a lunch on this particular day, and we set off in search of the perfect picnic spot. As my husband will attest to, this is no easy task. I am very picky about my picnic points. Not just any old spot will do. More goes into locating the spot than choosing the vittles. As any expert picnicker knows, the locale can make or break the entire expedition.

We drove down river several miles, my husband waiting patiently as his hunger pains rumbled loudly.

"How about this spot?" he optimistically asked again and again. But the silence spoke volumes.

Finally, after miles of searching, the perfect place was spotted. "Here! Stop the car!" I screamed.

It was glorious. Huge rocks lined the riverbed. Rolling rapids allowed the river to sing its sweet soothing song as it chugged along. The branches of spruce trees, laden with soft needles, laced the embankment providing a spot of shade. The sheer sandstone cliffs across the river shot high into the sky, a historical reminder of what had been, long before the forceful fluid carved its course.

Of course, there were ants. But on this day, at this glorious moment, amidst such abundant beauty, even the ants were welcome guests at our gathering. I offered them a piece of bread and they were satisfied, not invading what had not been offered.

The serene setting provided much needed peace. For the first time in a long time, I was quite content, sitting there soaking in all of the abounding beauty. Relaxing. Eating. Listening. Looking. Life was truly good. I was about to comment on the restful and relaxing atmosphere when suddenly a loud noise pierced the peacefulness. It came out of nowhere. Racket resonating off the cliffs. It was the shrill of screams. People laughing. The barking of orders.

"Paddle! Paddle, hard right! Harder," the commander bellowed. Then we could see it, the bright banana-colored raft coming our way. It was full of young girls. Except for the pending problem of the colossal boulder strategically situated squarely in the middle of their path, they seemed to be having fun. The navigational skills and courage of the occupants were about to be tested, in a big and dangerous way.

We had a bird's-eye view. I waited and watched. The ominous obstacle split the river only feet from where we sat. Would they hit or would they successfully, and safely, navigate the raft around the wretched rock? My husband and I held our breath and watched from the sidelines, cheering for the underdogs as they paddled to a barrage of loud and relentless instructional orders.

"Hard right! Paddle! Paddle! Harder!" the captain continued until the tranquil waters greeted their elongated tube. The raft had made it to calmer waters. With the skill of Navy sailors, the little women, weighing less collectively than the guide, had managed to paddle professionally past the peril. Once out of danger there was nothing left for them to do but sit back, rest, and relax while drifting slowly downstream in the sleepy waters.

Watching the adventure unfold before me created an emotional rainbow. Unable to be on that raft, and part of the rowing team, I was blue. However I realized how fortunate I was to be at that spot with the man who loves me so deeply. Focusing on my gift I lightened and brightened.

We finished our picnic, packed up our belongings and bid farewell to our perfect picnic spot. Reluctantly we strolled back to the car and onward we went, singing that famous song, our traveling tune: on the road again, just can't wait to get on the road again.

And hit the road we did, rolling constantly over pavement, pebbled paths through the mountains and flatlands of the Colorado countryside. Our feet rarely hit the ground; our heads barely hit a bed. I feared the tread on our vehicle would soon tire and wear thin. Yet, it was such an exciting and unique experience. Each dawn delivered a surprise, a gift waiting to be unwrapped.

It was midway into our trip when we happened upon a "Poke-n-plum" town. By the time you poke your head out the car window to see it, you're plum past it. It was here that I experienced a first (and at my age, a first of any type is always welcome). Being the ardent traveler I profess to be, it may seem strange that I have never experienced a Bed & Breakfast. Then again, given my wayward traveling ways, the B&B international organization would probably ban me.

My purpose in travel never alters. It is solely for leisure and pleasure, leaving behind the daily horrors of home life— the rebounding of missed laundry basket-bound socks and boxers, the removal of toothpaste spackling from the bathroom mirror, towel retrieval, and all other tidbits of tidiness. During travel, I eagerly toss aside the title of Domestic Goddess, crown myself the reigning Miss Piggy and indulge in the luxury of laziness. This Piggy persona is not conducive to the warm and friendly accommodations of a B&B. It is too up-close and personal for me, too revealing for everyone involved. On vacations I don't want to bond. I want to blend among and meld into the unknown masses. The shield of anonymity is necessary for this traveler who relishes the opportunity of throwing towels on the bathroom floor and then checking out before the dirty deed is discovered.

I lacked the desire to actually pay someone, namely a complete stranger, for the privilege of staying in their home, under their roof, and having to be on my best behavior all the time or risk getting thrown out on my ears. I am sure it is warm and wonderful for those *ain't misbehavin'* type travelers, but I like going undercover. What can I say? It is the only time I get to jump on a bed and throw towels around the room.

This time though, we were desperate, our choices were limited. Eager to make it a few more miles, we had pushed past the last city of any size many miles back. Now we found ourselves between this sleepy little village and breaking the fundamental law of scenic vacation vehicular travel—never driving past nightfall. Driving at dark, unable to see anything but the black of the night, defeats the whole purpose of tire transportation.

We entered the small community and drove the main drag in search of a room. No doubt it was the main drag because it was the only drag, the only road, and it wasn't really a road at all, but more of a well-worn dirt path. However, there was a hotel, a small and very expensive hotel. Not content, I pleaded for more options. While driving the half-mile thoroughfare, we noticed a woman by the road busy weeding her garden while simultaneously talking with a neighbor. A woman after my own heart, obviously gifted in both gab and gardening.

"Wait! Stop," I commanded. The sudden sound startled my driver husband. "Undoubtedly a local, she would be a wealth of information on this area."

Rolling down the car window, I rudely interrupted the neighborly exchange.

"Excuse me. How far is it to the next town, or would you

tell us where we can find a place close by to stay the night?" I pleasantly inquired.

"Well, it is about an hour's drive, but I have a bed and breakfast right here behind me and it is far better than any place around. I just happen to have a room available," she grinned as if snaring yet another desperate vacationer.

Just my luck, the one person I picked to ask just happens to own a B&B. How was I going to politely get out of this mess?

"Well we were hoping to be a little farther down the road by today. We will think about it. How much is your room any way?"

"I charge $100 per night which includes a sit-down breakfast," she answered.

I thanked her and motioned my husband to get us out of there quickly, before we became cornered. Back we went to the hotel to view a room. It was okay, but just mediocre, not deserving of the dollars they demanded. We weighed our options. And there were not many—the highway, the hotel, or the house.

It had been a long, hard day of travel, covering many miles that were crammed full of fun. Now we were tired. Our nerves were frazzled and it was showing. We wanted rest, food, and a nice, soft bed. Now! So after a brief discussion, we opted for the B&B. After all, it was located on a small, crystal clear stream and the available room was creek-side. Although I could not see the white ripples of the water from our window, the sounds of the water raging over the rocks resonated from wall to wall. That type of music would lull me into a deep sleep. That alone would be worth the price of the accommodations.

It didn't take long for me to discover that my reservations of B&Bs were well-founded. As we walked through the door, the hostess (without the mostess of hospitality) greeted us. Unfortunately, our welcome seemed more like a warning. Immediately I began to discover the many differences between being a hotel customer and a guest renting a room from a haughty, overbearing homeowner.

She wasted no time in laying down the law and making certain we knew the matriarchal pecking order in her castle. As soon as we entered her domain, she noticed the large, 32-

ounce water jug in my hand which I was toting to my, rather her, room.

"Oh no. Leave that outside. I will bring water and glasses to your room," she snarled as if the thing had cooties and would contaminate her environment.

There was a sound and healthful reason I was carrying my personal water container on vacation. It was big and made it easy for me to keep track of how much water I consumed in a day. I had it down to a science; the container was a vital part of my daily routine. However, our hostess made it clear that the topic of my container entering her upstairs was not open for discussion. So my spouse pried my fingers from the plastic handle and very obligingly put it back inside the car. I was not a happy trooper, and there was an uneasy feeling welling up inside of me.

The lady of the house proceeded to give us a tour of her home. Once in our room, excitement overcame me. I ran to open the window, eager to see the sights and hear the sounds. However, my excitement turned to apprehension with the sound of the madam's thundering footsteps coming across the room towards me. Our hostess descended upon me and pushed me aside.

"Here, let me do that! This is the *correct* way to properly open the blinds, curtains, and the windows," her tutorial tone sent chills down my spine.

The room was decorated straight from the pages of Town & Country magazine, with gold bathroom faucets and a matching gold shower head in her refurbished claw porcelain tub (emphasis on refurbished antique claw and delicate porcelain). She made it a point to explain precisely how to, and more importantly, how not to take a bath in her tub.

"Be careful to not let the showerhead lay in the bathtub, for it will scratch the porcelain," she said. "And don't push the shower curtain back too far . . . and make certain you don't get the lace curtain in the water. I will remove the comforter from the bed and get you a blanket," she rambled off her dictates. "Tell me what time you want your breakfast. It is not a continental breakfast, it's a real breakfast, and I personally prepare everything. So I need to know precisely when you want to eat so it can be ready."

She left, returning shortly with a crystal carafe of water and two glasses (not of the plastic sort) on a tray. She placed it in its proper place on the bedside table and bid us a good night. With the close of the door came my sigh of relief, then a rapid succession of bitching, moaning, and groaning.

"Oh, this is really nice. She really has a way of making one feel comfortable. Are we too uncivilized for a comforter? Who does she think she is?"

My husband just shrugged and headed for the head. I secretly hoped when we left he would leave the ring up. That would surely piss her off.

So went our relaxing evening. I was paranoid to move about in our room. Touching anything was off-limits, and lounging around was a scary thought too. Crinkled cushions would have surely tipped off our unruly behavior. I found myself tiptoeing upstairs so as not to disturb the homeowners located one floor below. I couldn't wait for morning to arrive so we could leave what I called the M&M, the matriarch and her museum. It reflected her immaculate and stylish taste, but not the warm, friendly comfort of a home.

However, it was rest we were after and rest we got. We were both fast asleep as soon as our heads hit the pillows. The next morning I woke early. Carefully I slipped out of bed, leaving my husband to his slumber. I woke early in order to get to the water's edge and greet the morning properly, with a hot cup of coffee and thankful meditation. I longed to witness the sun as it peeked over the crest of the blazing, red cliffs along the stream. I wanted to slowly and gently come to life, waking to the mist of the creek greeting my face.

A cup of coffee and I'd be on my way. Once I turned the kitchen corner, I saw her. Very kindly I inquired as to the whereabouts of the java. I was so browbeaten and scared by morning that I asked very little of the hostess for fear of setting her off or imposing upon her. Just one little cup of coffee is all I wanted.

"I have to make it. I don't drink coffee, so I don't make it unless you ask for it, and you didn't ask for it last night," she said as she opened the cabinet doors and pulled out the coffee maker.

I waited and waited, and then opted to escape the loud sound of the silence and head outdoors.

I walked to the back door and attempted to open the ornate glass French doors. I could feel her beady eyes inspecting my every move, so I was very careful—and very paranoid. One pull of the doorknob and nothing happened. Another attempt proved fruitless. Wouldn't you know it; I couldn't manage to get the darn doors open.

I knew what was about to happen. Then I heard it. Her footsteps coming quickly in my direction, each step sounding heavily on the wooden floor. I didn't know whether to duck or dodge.

"Don't do that anymore! I don't know what you have done," she snapped. "I will try," and that she did. Only she succeeded where I had failed.

Once the door was open, the hostess curtly handed me my cup of coffee along with parting words: "Here, go on." With pleasure, I obliged.

Oh, what a way to start a day! I needed peace and knew just where it lay. I sat on a large rock at the creek's edge watching, feeling and hearing the sights and sounds of the serenity before me. The mist was rising above the water; an eerie, white, puffy blanket magically hovering above the contents of the creek. The quietness was broken with the buzzing sounds of dive-bombing hummingbirds as they erratically zipped by on their quest for breakfast nectar at the nearby feeders.

The tension drained from my body as I watched the wonders of the cliff-lined valley come to life before me. It was truly glorious. Just as I had settled into my new, peaceful state, her bellowing beckoned me back to breakfast. I hated to give this up for that, but I couldn't let my husband suffer alone.

The dining table was set in a style suitable for a formal affair. Every utensil (and there were many) was in its proper place: juice glasses and water glasses were set perfectly above the elegant china plates topped with fancy folded cloth napkins. In another place at another time it would have been extraordinaire, but we were in the wilderness of the rugged Rocky Mountains, not in the Tavern on The Green restaurant in Central Park.

However, this was her place and her thing, and as a guest I was compelled to go along, and kept my mouth shut. I'm not a picky eater; there is little I won't eat. And wouldn't you know it. Breakfast consisted of the one dish I dislike. French toast is something I normally pass on. This time it was down the hatch with a smile and an approving, appreciative nod.

During the breakfast conversation I became really ill at ease noticing our hostess spoke directly to my husband as if I was not even in the room. They conversed during the entire breakfast in a civilized, even congenial repartee. He mentioned my recent surgery, and she pursued that topic, actually addressing me, and offering some unsolicited advice.

"Your body has gone through a drastic change, a major ordeal, and it will take a long time for you to completely heal," she said revealing the story of a friend who also had a recent hysterectomy. The point of her story, and her advice, was something I would not forget.

"Embrace the moment," she said repeatedly. "Enjoy this time. Just embrace this time of your life."

Yeah right! I would remember that every time I grasped my stomach in pain. From that moment on, that woman haunted the remainder of my recovery. With every ache, every shooting pain that pierced my body I heard her words echo through my mind: embrace the moment. Later, as I lay in bed, with my tummy in tremendous agony, I actually thought of paying her another visit just so I could pull her hair out. Yeah, right. Embrace this, I thought to myself as I imagined our tearful reunion.

When the steam stopped pouring forth from my ears, I was able to understand the true meaning of her message. As much as I hate to admit it, she was right in her theory. A woman, after undergoing a hysterectomy or any other life-altering surgery, must seize the opportunity to nurture herself and allow ample time for recovery, recuperation and rejuvenation.

Bearing the Big H

How rare is the occasion when a woman is the center of attention; the one that is doted on instead of doing the doting; the one pampered instead of pampering. A time when the best medicine is rest and relaxation, complete with bubble baths and, scented candles. Recovery is a time when the best trip may be an inward journey, to revisit, rejuvenate, realign the soul; to see the inner-self in a new light, with deeper dimension and better understanding.

SIXTEEN

Cringe & Bare It

No doubt about it: Time has certainly taken its toll on my love life. My romantic side has gone by the wayside. What was once a burning flame is now an occasional flicker. This sad fact was not the result of any surgery. No, it had more to do with life, the learning process, costly lessons, thirty years of mistakes. It had to do with accumulating a vast wealth of experience during attempts to locate the mythical Mr. Right. Need I say more?

It is ironic that when I finally found, and eventually got my hooks into him, my wanton desires have turned to wantin' nothing! My Mr. Right now suffers for all my years of failed fairytales and nightmarish encounters.

Sad but true, my amour is no more. My romantic, candlelight dinners, complete with soft music and hours of sweet desserts served in the bedroom, have definitely changed. Now the menu consists of hamburgers served on the patio with two dogs at our feet begging for a morsel of food. Our bed is shared with two mutts and sometimes as many cats. The soft music has given way to sounds of purring and/or growling. Our children have full access to the king-size bed and always prefer to snuggle closely to their parents so that room on the huge mattress is reduced to that of a one-man cot.

This all provides another excuse for not fully, completely indulging in the sex scene. How can we *do it* when we have no privacy? When and if those rare desires surface, the glare and stare of our accompanying canine critters burn holes in the mood. If that doesn't douse the flame, the slurping, licking, and scratching serenade from their grooming always snuffs the romantic mood. Our bedroom is just not conducive to intimacy.

It wouldn't matter if we were alone anyway. Things still wouldn't boogie much in the bedroom. For me, foreplay consists of one thing—asking the question: Honey, do you want on top or bottom this time?

My husband has been trying to convince me that love-making is not a spectator sport but one that requires participation. He should have been able to read the writing on the wall during our honeymoon. On our wedding night I fell asleep immediately after he knocked my socks off, which unfortunately for him was before he received the much-anticipated "honey" part of the honeymoon. It was more of a honey-moan, for he groaned and moaned and has never let me forget it, or live down that one small failure. I think he likes to hold it over my head as a little guilt trip when he is pleading with me to participate in our current sporting event.

I am laying groundwork for my point here. Many patients are warned one of the side effects of this surgery and the ensuing hormone replacement therapy is loss of sexual drive. Yeah, like I had much to begin with! My sexual drive (stuck in reverse) could more adequately be described as a sexual drag.

At least surgery provided me with a good excuse. I love excuses. They are as valuable to me as gold bullion, and just as difficult to obtain now that I am without PMS and the sorts. Mention headaches, cramps, PMS, or menstrual flow to a man, and his response will probably be one of two: "Here we go again" or "Oh, that's just a woman's thing!"

Of course, there is a big difference between a woman's things and a man's things. This operation allowed me to learn another distinction between the two, like I needed any more. During recovery I realized firsthand the most significant difference between genders. I have always said women are emotional and men are physical. (I often wonder if I were to lose my breasts if my husband could still hold me). Women like to converse, communicate and commiserate; men like to connect, contact, and commingle.

There is, of course, a special womanly bond among us females, and that bond seems to strengthen among us surgically menopausal types. Whether a long-time friend, a recent encounter, or an interlude with a stranger on the street, women are ever so compassionate when they meet another that has endured the same. So unlike the male counterparts, who for the most part, pout and indulge in self-pity as their wives recover and try to regain a normal life. Many males are just unable, incapable of relating to any womanly woes.

However, men must be given their dues. The poor souls also go through a recuperation period of sorts following a wife's hysterectomy. Only the male version consists of complaining and counting the weeks, days, and hours until the infamous D.R.D. This anxiously-awaited, eagerly-anticipated moment is, of course, the doctor's release day—the green light, go-ahead to resume normal relations, which for those male physical beings means one thing: sex! It's the time the husband can unleash his pent-up frustration, which has accumulated during the long, abstinent weeks of recovery.

The year before I underwent the Big H my boss's wife had surgery. Although he did not confide the nature of her operation to his subordinates, women's intuition told us that she was about to rid herself of the source of some womanly worries.

My employer remained rather rational during much of the ordeal. Working in the pressure cooker of a newsroom, he somehow maintained an undaunted disposition. I commended him on the fact that he did not allow his personal circumstances to interfere with his professionalism. However, at week number six, his docile demeanor took a disappointing downward turn, his even keel got off-kilter. Before our very eyes, in a matter of moments, he transformed into a real monster, a beast at best. The slightest inconvenience, the smallest mistake sent him reeling into a boisterous outward expression of his frustration (of course, the key word here is frustration).

On those occasions I, like many of my colleagues, did not understand what had sent our fearless and tranquil leader into such fits of rage. Little did I know then that one year later I would be walking in his wife's shoes and my own husband would be trudging down that same celibate path as my former boss. Only then was I able to grasp an understanding of his plight and the probable origin of my editor's rampages. Doing the math, making a calendar comparison I would venture to guess it had to do with *that time* that pivotal point, the sixth week of recovery, when the male trans-forms from the caring spouse into the deprived husband. In other words, he's horny.

Men and women alike count the days from the date of surgery until the doctor's release day. If all goes according to schedule for the fledgling female patient, it is forty-two glori-ous, uninterrupted days without being pursued, hounded, mauled, or pawed! For their counterparts, the men pass the time by eagerly waiting, gazing at the calendar, and count-ing down the days all the while fantasizing, anticipating, and foaming at the mouth like some wild, starved wolf ready for the privilege to pounce on the unsuspecting lamb.

During this season of solitude, I found that threaten-ing a relapse works wonders in keeping a spouse in line and at bay. Whatever the situation, this hint always seemed to get my husband's attention, and I played the tune often to pull his strings.

"Oh, you don't feel like helping me with the housework? You really think I have healed enough to vacuum the whole house by myself?" I would ask my mate. "Well, I'll try, but if I pull anything, then my doctor may tell me to refrain from all physical activity again, and you know what that means."

It is amazing how fast a man can move with the right motivation. To be honest, my husband would like an oppor-tunity to tell his side of this story. My reply to him is simply: write your own book!

Speaking of sexual activity, some may be wondering what, if any, effect the Big H actually has on a woman's libido. When can one get back to the basics of life and love-making? And there are probably even more women wonder-ing how long they can use the Big H as an excuse to dodge their wifely duty.

Well, there are two methods used to calculate the time frame for resuming sexual relations, the doctor's and the patient's. For some unknown reason, they vary vastly.

Routinely doctor's orders state no sexual intercourse for six weeks following surgery. My six-week point was marked by yet another postoperative appointment. For me it was a day that will live in infamy. Before my very eyes my husband turned from a concerned caregiver to a puberty-panicked, testosterone-inflicted, sex-starved, teenage horn dog. Several weeks of celibacy had definitely taken its toll on him, and my healing body was about to bear the brunt of all those sexless days and nights.

I was barely off the examining table and into the lobby before my husband's thoughts shifted from paying the doctor to playing a doctor. We were not even out the door of the gynecologist's office when he let his desires be known. Without pausing for an answer, my husband jumped from, "How was the doctor's visit?" to "Can we do it now?"

The lapse in our lovemaking had apparently caused a lapse in his rational thinking. More likely he was thinking with some organ other than (and located opposite of) his brain! Although seriously flawed, his reasoning was so simple—and so male. I couldn't believe my ears as he gave his rationale for getting on with life, i.e., *getting it on.*

"If the doctor's instruments didn't bother you, then lovemaking wouldn't cause pain either." Who but a man (and a caveman at that) would have deduced that?

The man before me was not the loving, kind, compassionate man I had married. No, something had definitely happened over the past several weeks. It was becoming obvious the surgery, or rather the recovery, had a dramatic effect on my other half as well.

He was afflicted by a male virus that causes sex on the brain. His focus shifted, his thoughts were limited to one thing, even his vocabulary was affected. He was possessed and began using words I never heard him utter before. Words best reserved for seedy romance novels. This was evident during a relentless Mike Wallace-style interview. His third-degree line of questioning was the result of my reluctance to succumb to his pleas, pressure, and playfulness.

"Why don't you want to make love? What are you afraid of? Are you frightened about me entering you or afraid of the thrust?" he questioned and queried.

I couldn't believe my ears, or the descriptive wording used by my once shy husband. I didn't know whether to cry, laugh, or start mental commitment proceedings. I was certain of only one thing (and he made no bones about it) he was suffering from that strange male disease called "lackanookie."

He was overcome by passion. His physical need (as opposed to desire) had gotten the best of him. But I couldn't feel sorry for my husband. He had been without for only six weeks, but this surgery had rendered me without for a lifetime. Gone was my reliable reason for going to bed with only the intimacy of a good book. With the removal of my built-in excuse, I would be subjected to a life without my cherished once-a-month, weeklong sabbatical.

Unbeknownst to my husband, my periods were getting longer as he got hornier. Now I was faced with nothing to save me but the last few savoring minutes of recovery. And had it not been for the meddling of my male gynecologist, they would have lasted even longer.

It wasn't that I completely lacked all desire to make love to my husband; it was that fear dampened all desire. The painful thought of him mingling among my still-recovering inner parts was too much for me to willingly submit my body to! However, my surgical excuse was no exception to the old rule that all good things must come to an end. And end it did, but not like I had envisioned.

The timing couldn't have been more perfect. Twice a year, every year my husband and I travel back into time on a sentimental journey to our honeymoon haven. Nestled in the mountainous woods overlooking a lake, the beauty that surrounds this cottage is surpassed only by the peacefulness and seclusion it provides its guests. This is where we had taken our marriage vows. Something about that place affects me like no other. Whether it is the fresh mountain air, the seclusion, the lack of interference from the outside world, no television or telephone, or just the nostalgia that comes over me when we return to the place where we vowed to love one another until death do us part, I don't know for sure. One thing I do know (as does my husband), it brings the wild thing out in me. And it makes my husband's heart sing, too.

On the same day as the doctor's release day we celebrated our second anniversary. In honor of the occasion, we embarked upon the four-hour trip into the neighboring magical mountains. My husband's planning was perfect, he knew how and where to best get what he wanted most. Oh, I knew sooner or later submission would win out; and I feared the time was now, no getting around it.

Although he had driven hours after putting in a full day at the office, my mate was as energetic and determined as a dog trailing a rabbit. Once cornered, my testosterone-driven, hound-dog hunting of a husband wasted no time in getting down to business.

He was amorous and oh-so excited, full of energy and raring to go. I, on the other hand, was just tense. Oh so tense. I had this horrible fake grin painted on my pale face and the veins on my forehead were bulging. Within minutes of crossing the threshold, he was on me like a starved woodpecker attacking a hollowed tree.

A willing participant I was not. My body and mind were on separate courses. My head may have said yes, but my body objected vehemently, and it showed. I was paralyzed with fear. My legs seemed to be super-glued together. And for good reason, after all, it had been mere hours since my doctor had invaded with his torturous tools. The thought of being entered twice in the same afternoon was more than I could fathom.

Although physically able (according to my male doctor), I was neither ready nor willing, and the closer the moment, and movement got, the more obvious that fact became to my husband! Regardless of the pitiful facial expressions or the undeniable body language, the moment had come, or was about to. This interlude was anything but romantic. At my insistence we dispensed with the foreplay. On this occasion it was viewed as a torture tactic used to prolong the agony. I had not one romantic notion or motion. Quick and painless was my only concern, getting it on and getting it over. It was as romantic as making love in a feedlot.

There was no stopping him now. Within a split second, before I could even attempt a stiff arm, or plead my case for patience, there he was right in front of me, right on top of me and in my face. Where or how was I to run now?

Moreover, what good would it have done? It had to happen some day. It is just part of the mating game.

I held my legs tightly together as he pushed forward. He was determined to try, and I was determined to deny. I was petrified. He was close, oh-so close. I could feel him inching even closer to his destination. The moment was fast approaching, no wiggling out now. My body stiffened. Then suddenly the forward motion stopped, the tension eased. He was lingering on top of me, and staring intently into my eyes.

"Why are you grimacing? I haven't even gotten through the leg barricade. I haven't done anything yet! Are you hurting?"

The only word I could manage through gritted teeth and a clinched jaw was "Nah."

"Then why are you grimacing?" he repeated.

"Cause I just know what's coming."

I must not have been pitiful enough, for he kept on keeping on. With no more excuses and no real pain to stop the action, the moment arrived. I took a deep breath, held it, and hoped that the speculum the doctor had used earlier was the most painful thing I would encounter this day! And then I felt it.

Hello Houston. I think we have contact, was the only thing that went through my mind.

Then to put a real damper on the moment I said something I had never uttered before (although the thought may have crossed my mind a time or two). "Can't you just hurry up?"

That romantic question didn't faze his quest, or slow his rhythm. During the brief encounter it was apparent his focus was on his relief and not my grief.

"Am I hurting you?" he asked, without missing a beat (no pun intended).

But there wasn't enough time to answer. Going for weeks without had one positive impact. Luckily, it was over almost before it started.

Although he had honored my request and performed in record time, the hormonal hellion kicked into overdrive and seized one last opportunity to make a jab, inflict more pain and do more damage before mounting my broomstick and fleeing the room.

Before he had time to even open his eyes and savor the second, I blurted out the unbelievable. "Now get off me!" I hissed.

So much for the gory details of our first postsurgical interlude. After release of his frustrations, I expected my sweet husband to resurface. However, that didn't happen. It wasn't my husband but a complete stranger that spoke as soon as he rolled off and over.

"Well, the first time had to come sometime and we got that out of the way." Then he added another comment, a word of which I couldn't hear. He either said, "I am glad we got past that dramatic event," or he said, "I am glad we got past that traumatic event."

I hate to compare sex with a doctor's appointment; but like my earlier visit that day, I discovered that the most painful part was the anticipation. I don't honestly believe my husband ever understood or fully comprehended an important point regarding that fateful first fling following surgery. On that particular day, I had not one but two men invading my tender body for two entirely different reasons. One obviously was for a medically sound reason, and necessary. The other however, was mentally unsound and physically driven by a one-track mind, which by its very nature, is almost always off course.

Two invasive procedures within one day was more than any woman would want or should be expected to endure in such a short span. It would have been so much nicer had there been some time between vaginal visitations.

Patience is an important principle the first year following surgery. I highly recommend erecting a bright yellow yield sign above the bed that reads: YIELD-Patience for the patient

This initial interlude did provide an opportunity to ask a looming question. It wasn't long after surgery I began to wonder what any normal woman might wonder. I wanted to know if I felt any different internally. It's never been said that I am a shy person. And whom better to ask such a personal question than the one who knows best. And now that he had done the research, I saw no reason to procrastinate or beat around the bush. I am fully aware of the experts' advice regarding those precious moments following the climactic event, the time best reserved for holding and hugging. However, I seized the moment to size up my insides. Forget the timing, the poor man was caught totally off guard by my bluntness and boldness.

"Honey, do I feel any different now that I am hollow? Can you tell when we make love?"

That poor man. My dear, dear husband. Marriage to me was certain to guarantee him a place in heaven. First there was the PMS, then the pain. Now the surgery followed by the ensuing disgusting questions.

When we married he was a reserved, shy kind of guy. I guess it's true what they say about opposites attracting. Bit by bit, one bold inquiry after another, he was transforming. No topic is off conversational limits as far as I'm concerned. He was learning firsthand what he always suspected was true: women like to discuss everything and discuss it to pieces.

However, in his wildest nightmares, I am sure he never expected to be confronted with the ultimate: a hormonal-crazed wife asking an asinine question, which would cause him grief no matter what his response. Once he regained his composure, you could hear the wheels turning inside his head as he assessed the situation. After weighing his words carefully, in a gentle, loving tone, he spoke sincerely straight from his heart.

"No, Dear. You are the woman I married, the woman you have always been, the woman I love. No organ can make you, no surgery could ever change you."

Wow! Talking about scoring some postoperative points. Okay, so maybe he deserves a break for that one.

SEVENTEEN

Menopausal Moments

The ink wasn't even dry on the surgical consent forms when the effects of my hysterectomy began trickling down through my life, haunting me in one form or fashion. For some reason most of them centered on age. Why age? I asked myself time and time again. What was the correlation between me, my surgery and my maturity? Maybe it was just a mental, psychological, or an emotional thing. I mean lets get real here. Age and aging is not relative, does not relate to, nor is it impacted by a hysterectomy. I know! I am certain! I did the research on the subject! Remember? I can't find any such silliness in any medical data or journals.

Just because a woman looses her ability to bear children is no indication she is sliding fast and furious headfirst down the hill of life. In my little mind I was still climbing upward and onward, toward the peak. And as far as I was concerned, I was a long way from cresting that prime peak of life. But this hysterectomy thing leads me in a whole different direction. Was being barren a sign of being on the descent and, therefore, over the hill? Everything that happened after surgery sure pointed in that pivotal position.

My first age spot was discovered just a few weeks after the Big H. I never imagined in my wildest dreams one of those things on my lovely, youthful skin. And who else but my loving spouse would take pleasure in pointing out such a ghastly discovery? It was over dinner that the eye-opening mark was first detected.

"Honey look, this spot on my hand is new. I think a freckle has popped up. Maybe I am in the sun too much and should wear gloves when working in the yard," I naively spoke.

Thinking it was nothing more than another sun kiss,

I modeled it for my husband, waving my hand here and there, letting it float gently by his face, slowing only to afford him the opportunity to admire my delicate hand, complete with its newest beauty mark.

First he shrugged me and my new speck off, nonchalantly glancing from his dinner plate to the wavering hand in front of his face. He seemed uninterested and hadn't given me the attention I wanted, and demanded! I didn't know when I was well off. Seeing that the topic of my hand had not captured his full attention as it (and we) deserved, I foolishly continued the conversation, and pressed further.

"Will you look here and admire my latest little brown beauty, please!" I pleaded while pointing to the little fellow.

The subject would not be dropped, nor would the hounding cease until he acted as if he cared. He reluctantly reached across the table and took my hand for a closer inspection. I could see the alarming smirk as it emerged across his face, growing from ear to ear. Oh, how I knew that look. I readied myself for the punch.

"Dear, that is not a freckle or even a mole. Congratulations! You have your first age spot," he announced without even batting an eye and while scooping the last morsel of food from his plate and shoveling it into his *overly large* mouth. His pointed comment had pierced my pride.

"No way. You are just saying that," I argued.

But he pleaded his case with physical evidence, holding out his own age-spotted hand. One would think that in my delicate hormonal condition he would have gone along with my opinion, regardless of its inaccuracy.

Boy, I tell you it was just another example of how husbands foolishly take their lives in their own hands by testing their wive's temperament. After I reinflated my deflated fragile ounce of ego, I spent the rest of the evening in a trance, staring at my new age spot trying to determine the difference between a freckle and the other, more demeaning descriptive alter-ego.

Was there a distinction? Is one darker than the other? Is one bigger or brighter? Do freckles have a more symmetrical shape than age spots? How does one really know which is which? How often will they pop up and how many should be expected during one's life? Is there a formula for calculating how many will appear, an age spot for every decade of life? Or do they appear haphazardly and on a whim? Will they fade with the passage of time? Does medication eradicate this telltale sign of aging, or are gloves destined to become a permanent ensemble to my wardrobe? And why in the world would anyone (other than a husband) ever want to admit to having one? Can't all discoloration be labeled as freckles? So many questions and so much to worry about with this aging thing.

To add insult to injury and make matters even worse (if that indeed was possible) the very next day the mail brought more bad news, yet another sorrowful and painful reminder of my true age. A trip to the mailbox is always an adventure for me, like having a daily surprise party. Sometimes the result is cause for a celebration, finding a card, cheerful note, or some much anticipated correspondence. More often than not, however, the bad news outweighs the good. Anxiety and aggravation develop as piles of bills, advertisements, and junk mail stream forth from the opened box. Sometimes I am tempted to just leave my worries behind, slam the mailbox shut, and walk away empty-handed.

However, as I was about to learn, there are some things worse than creditor's correspondence. I was not prepared for the news that the postman carried in his little mailbag this particular afternoon. Full of anticipation, I hurried to the mailbox. Once inside, a personal letter was discovered. Thrilled and overly anxious, I began guessing the contents.

"This has just gotta be good, maybe another get well wish from a concerned friend, or someone sending their best wishes for a speedy recovery," I was just elated at the prospects.

It had been a while since my surgery. It was that awful, stagnant period between surgery and full recovery when the only concern left is from the patient herself. Therefore, this card was to be a cause for celebration! The excitement was overwhelming. Eagerly I tore open the correspondence.

First a little peek. Then a closer inspection. And then nothing but a blank stare. Once the contents registered, my chin dropped, my mouth hung open. There it was in black and white, no mistaking the markings. It was an invitation to my twentieth high school reunion. Me? No way! There had to be a mistake. Feverishly I checked the addressee. Although maiden, it was my name.

How can a woman who "claims" to be in her early thirties possibly have a twentieth high school reunion? It is a mathematical impossibility. Tenth or fifteenth reunion maybe, but not the big double dime.

I checked again. No doubt about it—my high school, my name, my twentieth. Now, high school reunions, by their very nature, cause people to do two things. First, they must admit to growing older. Like it or not, receiving an invitation to my twentieth high school reunion signaled I was aging—in the direction opposite of which I claimed and calculated.

Secondly, it causes a person (especially us vain dames) to look in the mirror. You must understand what type of gander I am referring to. I am not talking about the "psychological babble" which a shrink uses when attempting to get a patient to look inward. No, that type of examination is certainly too deep a topic for me to tackle. I am referring to a shallower glance in the mirror, one focusing on appearance. Sure enough, what I saw staring back at me was a face full of its fair share of wisdom lines. (Not wrinkles I remind you, but wisdom lines for those of us still in age denial).

I could take the surgical menopause even though the word menopause (regardless of whatever adjective was attached) has aging connotations. I could even take a hint of a very SMALL age spot. And taken alone, the high school reunion could have signaled the success of making it this far in life. But all three at the same time was more this ole woman could bear. Talk about a real big dose of reality, of a very great magnitude, all in a very small time frame.

It was much too much to take all at once. It was overwhelming. My head was spinning and my legs wobbled. Quickly I searched for a chair to rest my now weary (and now old) soul. Later that night I mustered the nerve to take a closer look at myself in the mirror to make certain something had not been overlooked. A different image was there this time. It was not the person I was accustomed to, but a stranger staring back—a woman holding an invitation with her blossoming age spots shining brightly; sagging boobs, pulled down by earth's gravity, pointed to a huge crimson scar that cut a path across her abdomen separating them from the area still shaven clean of pubic hair; a face adorned with wisdom lines and crow's feet with a blank look in her eyes.

If ever there was a time in which I was in need of a shrink and all that psychological babble, it was now! At the least, an IV, with a solution of both estrogen and Prozac, was certainly in order. No, wait! I could do this without drugs.

Okay, get a grip! You are getting older, no doubt about it. It is just a fact of life, I told the ghost in the mirror before me. Just deal with it!

A plan, I needed a plan for my golden years. Let me see, there were role models. Oh yeah, my mom. She had managed to grow old gracefully. She is more attractive and younger looking now than years past. I thought about her. How did she manage? Being a widow, she relied heavily on the company of her children. It had to be that my younger brother and I kept her laughing and young at heart. But if that was the secret, I was certainly in big trouble.

I never had children due to three different stages in my life—I wouldn't, I shouldn't, and then I couldn't. In all honesty, I had never really wanted children and was insightful and honest enough to recognize and admit this. I was too self-centered and independent to undertake such a big, lifelong endeavor. However, this thinking applied only while my baby-making mechanism was intact.

Things were different now. The precise moment my incubator organs were removed, everything suddenly centered on infants. Babies, babies, and more babies. They were everywhere! There was no escaping them. In the stores sitting in the grocery cart, on the streets riding in strollers, in a sling dangling from a parent's neck, peering from a backpack. The newspaper and television pictured, posed and paraded the little tykes in every form and fashion. From commercials to soap operas to sitcoms, I could not elude motherhood and childhood.

Figuring it would provide a much-needed break from

the baby-blues, I sought solace in my soap opera. Erica's love life would surely provide me with a reprieve. It was the first time in many months I had left reality in favor of daytime drama. And who would have thunk it? It was not shocking scandals, adulterous affairs or steamy sex scenes that appeared on the screen. Oh no! No, it was all about babies. One of the main characters had just given birth to a baby girl and in this particular episode was showing her off to everyone. I watched the sickening scene as grandma foamed at the mouth upon her first encounter with her new grandchild. And that wasn't all of it. It got even worse. Who else but a woman with a bad heart and one kidney manages to become pregnant? Enough already! That was the final straw!

Desperate to escape the deluge of the toddler topic, I flipped channels with record speed. However, there was no escape, not even the commercials were childproof. There must be thousands of types of diapers and millions of brands of formulas. I was being tortured, bombarded with baby babbling. My head was twirling. Everywhere it was children, conception, and/or childcare. The television had turned into an infant-marketing Mecca.

If it wasn't after the fact, it was before the fact. How many attempts, how many times, how many ways, how many tools, and how many colors does it take for a woman to know whether she is pregnant? Either she is or she isn't. End of story, end of commercial. Let's get on the down road.

Flipping onward, I finally found what seemed to be a safe bet, a sitcom called *Designing Women*. If memory serves me correctly, this show is centered on the lives of four single women. How safe could one get, with four singles? Only five minutes into the episode I discovered how wrong I was! Seems like a lot had happened since I last tuned into the show. One of the four had gotten married. And I was fortunate to bear witness to the cuddling and cooing episode.

The nightly news would certainly provide me a much-needed break. So focused on the depressing, disgusting, and demented, there was rarely time left for anything uplifting. But not this time, not when I tuned in. Would someone please explain why the local news station has nothing better to cover than a story on fertility and various methods used to become pregnant? This was newsworthy? Give me a break! Obviously it was a very slow news day.

Truth is, nothing had changed in the outside world. The alteration was internal, limited to my own little world. Sad to say, my biological clock didn't start ticking until after my chimes were removed. Now that it was too late, the ticking was clicking. Tick, tick, tick, tick—fast and furious it sounded.

This prompted a psychological transformation. My thoughts, my views, my attitude changed. No longer did I refer to infants and toddlers as cookie monsters, curtain climbers or my all-time favorite: rug rats. Children crying in public places had once sent me into a total fit of rage, but now they pulled out my heartstrings. Where I once pitied a woman piled down with diaper bags and screaming strollers, I found myself trying to sneak a peek to see the angelic eyes beneath the security of their soft baby blanket.

Longingly looking into infants' eyes the severity and impact of having a hysterectomy hit me. I had never, nor would I ever, experience the true meaning, the ultimate feeling of womanhood—the pain, the agony and the ultimate joy of bringing forth a life from the womb into the world.

The full impact of this revelation did not take its toll until almost a year after surgery. Instead of postpartum depression, I suffered from postoperative depression. In my case, this condition made me a basket case and presented another excuse for my wacky ways. I had gone off the deep end and it was becoming apparent even to me. The warning signs were ignored until I began envying the nesting wren on our patio. The mother and her plight became my delight—and an obsession of sorts.

It was a ritual. Every morning while enjoying my coffee outside, I would watch mama wren as she hurriedly, and very professionally, constructed her nursery nest. When it was completed to her satisfaction, she sat, and I waited. The closer the due date, the more nervous we both became. She was flighty, more cautious of the comings and goings of her surroundings. I started pacing the patio waiting for the miraculous moment to arrive—the cracking of the shells, the emerging of the babies.

One afternoon my nervousness gave way to sadness. There on the concrete surface I discovered the tiny fragments of a shattered egg. This set me into a rage. It was outrageous and unacceptable for a maternity ward! It was time to take matters into my own hands. I ran into the house to tell my husband of my plans.

"Honey, something horrible has happened. Something has gotten into the wren's nest and is stealing her eggs," I explained my disgusting discovery. "I am going to stay outside, stand guard until I find out what kind of creature would do such a terrible thing. Once the perpetrator is caught, I will use what-ever means necessary to make certain it doesn't happen again to that poor, poor mama wren. She must be so distraught!"

My husband listened intently as I rambled on. Although accustomed to my weirdness, I had gone a little too far this time.

"My dear, poor, darling wife, there is nothing wrecking havoc on the wren's nest. In all likelihood, the mother bird threw the egg out of the nest herself and probably for a very good reason," he tried to soothe my shattered nerves. "They have a way of knowing when something isn't right with an egg and so they push it out on purpose. It's instinct."

Oh, so that was it. Okay. I got over the destroyed egg, but not over the family scene unfolding before my very eyes on my very patio. I was so excited. Each day I awoke won-dering if this would be the big day. Then finally it happened. A baby wren came into being. The proud chirps of both mom and dad made the occasion known to everything within earshot. However, the celebration was short-lived as the real work of raising an offspring began.

The parents were so busy the first week finding the perfect insect, catching, and then transporting it across the yard back to the nest, into the crib and finally forcing it down the baby's beak. They were the perfect set of parents, sharing the parental chores, including the dirty jobs. Routinely mom and dad would duck inside the nest, carry the poop piles away in their beaks, and then deposit them on our patio for proper and permanent disposal.

I was jealous of their joy and envied mom, secretly

wishing to be in her parental place. Knowing that would never happen, I had no option but to accept my new role as grandmother. I was content to watch my grandbirdie from afar. Every day, the family scene beckoned me, drawing me back again and again.

As the baby got its wings it started leaving the nest more often, and for longer periods. Inevitably things on the home front changed. Mom became more attentive, more intense and nervous. Her chirps, louder and sharper, could be heard more often as she instructed and scolded her growing child. Dad didn't come around as often, content with leaving the raising part to the other parent. I figured he was out having a beer with his buddies, happy to be out of the way.

Then one day baby birdie left the nest for good perching nearby. I thought about catching it and stuffing it back into the safety of its nest, with some forceful words of wisdom. You are only young once. Take advantage of this time in your life. You have the rest of your life to leave the nest. Don't rush things. It's a cold, hard world out there!

Remembering myself at that age when I left my own nest, I knew the effort would have been for naught. Like me that wisdom would have gone in one ear and quickly out the other. At that adolescent age the brain hasn't developed enough to fill the emptiness between the ears, absorb the advice.

Day after day, I closely and quietly watched the baby grow up. Clad only in a sparse array of down, it maneuvered through the vines of the wisteria, all the while mom chirping orders, and offering motherly advice. The chirping never ceased, growing louder the farther the baby ventured away from home. Although the baby left its perch, I was able to track its whereabouts thanks to the signaling shrills of mom.

Then the sounds stopped. Silence and stillness returned to the patio. My coffee breaks were void of the familiar sights and sounds I had grown to love and anticipate with the dawning of each new day. The excitement and enjoyment derived from my new residents was replaced with an emptiness, sadness, and depression. The empty-nest syndrome had hit home.

Things escalated after I lost my fine, feathered family of friends. I was suffering from postpartum depression which became all too apparent while walking my dogs along the shores of the nearby lake. It was a glorious morning, the air was fresh and crisp, and the birds were singing their songs. I was in rare form, full of vigor and vitality. I sat down on a rock and watched as the dogs frolicked in the water. Then a stone about two inches long there at my feet caught my eyes.

It was an unusual color, the red sandstone contrasting a softer pale yellow. As I picked it up for a closer look, the stone changed to a figurine—the image so distinct, clear and obvious. It was a mother, holding a baby in her arms and kissing it. My mind was playing tricks on me.

Attempting to clear the fuzz from my eyes, I blinked once, then twice and stared again, more intently this time. But there was no doubting the image. I held the rock tightly in my hands for a long time as tears trickled down my cheeks, and emptiness settled in my heart. I put the rock in my pocket for safekeeping. What a real treasure I had found.

I still have that rock, tucked safely away in my dresser drawer. I had to keep it not only for sentimental reasons but also for sanity's sake. The only thing that stood between the mental hospital and me was the obvious image found on that rock. But for that piece of stone my husband would have accused the surgeon of removing organs from the wrong end, brains instead of ovaries, performing a lobotomy instead of a hysterectomy.

Slowly I came to accept the fact there would be no joyous occasion of my own making or delivering. I calmed down and eventually my sanity returned . . . until the phone call came. It was our family lawyer reporting on the drafting of our last will and testament. The poor soul called only to ask a few simple questions, make certain everything was in order and correct before the final instrument was prepared.

"Let me see, you and your husband have no children? None from a previous marriage? Neither of you have any children?"

"No, no, and no," I answered calmly. So far so good.

"Well, then are any planned, on the way, or in the oven?"

Wrong question, wrong time, and wrong client! That was all this sterile, hysterical, hysterectomy-stricken woman needed to hear.

"NO!" I shouted into the phone. "My oven has been removed!" And with that, the conversation came to an abrupt end.

Later that evening, my husband suggested a night on the town, something to get my mind off things. For a long time we had promised my former boss and his wife we would go out to dinner with them. It seemed to be the perfect time for such an outing. So it was decided and the arrangements were made.

The four of us were sitting at our table enjoying a margarita, in celebration of his new career and recognition of my new anatomical status. In the middle of the toast a man approached our table. Although a stranger to me, he was a friend of our guests. My husband and I sat quietly while a conversation ensued between the three of them.

Whether too much to drink or to little in his head, what prompted the stranger's question remains a mystery to me. It was either bad tequila or a Freudian slip.

"Do you know about the latest hot flash?" he asked us all. The silence grew loud at our table. The cloud of shock lingered overhead. He simply talked on, without missing a beat but I didn't hear him. I was busy shaking my head; fine tuning my hearing; freeing the wax from my ears. No way I could have heard him right. Before I could question the man, he disappeared.

Whether he meant to say hot tip or news flash, I will never know for sure. The only thing I'm certain is no man in his right mind would be dumb enough to mention a menopausal matter to a group wherein two of the four had recently undergone a hysterectomy. I seriously doubt he meant to ask or wanted to know if we had had any hot flashes lately. That is a sacred subject, one most men avoid, many husbands vicariously experience, and many women discuss and cuss on a routine basis.

Seemed like the whole world was out of control these days. Blunders and babies; babies and blunders. It was strange how things started snowballing, revolving around and rolling down that hormonal hill once surgery was over and I became surgically menopausal. I guess hysteria hits after the hysterectomy!

EIGHTEEN

Hints Forth

Eeeeeeek. Pssshshshhhhhh. Whoa! I made it! Over the mountains, through the forest, across those ravines, safely and sanely I completed the tumultuous trek along the hysterectomy highway. It was a wild ride, and sometimes unpredictable. Yet it's done, finished, over with, in the past. Finally, I have jumped the fertile *herdle* and graduated from cyclical sick-o to wombless wonder. I have gained, and grown, for having made the trip. And surviving it all there are some surgery suggestions, recovery recommendations, life lessons worth noting.

HINT 1: Keep your eyes open. Watch the road. Focus on the journey's purpose.

For those in the driver's seat, it's important to remember a hysterectomy is a detour, not an obstacle. It's not just a surgery, but also a radical removal of organs. It is a transformation. And its impact isn't limited to the anatomy, but is all encompassing, influencing the mental, emotional, and psychological, in positive and negative ways.

Recovery is a time for coasting. It is a long, hard road, with many a winding turn. It is a time-consuming, energy-zapping, mood-altering process. Attitude can make or break the patient, hamper the healing, wreck the home life. Occasional attitude adjustments are vital for a safe trip and a smooth transition.

Most things are great in moderation, but in big doses even the heavenly can turn hellish. Sitting on your butt all day and taking it easy sounds wonderful—and don't get me wrong it is great, for a while anyway. Then it becomes a portentous pothole.

I had been forewarned and told to just sit back and relax by others. However, being the stubborn, impatient, and hardheaded woman (which I conveniently dismiss as a learning disability of sorts) I was slow to catch their drift. It took time, too much time, for me to comprehend, bend and mend my ways. So heed the warning: SLOW! Dangerous conditions exist along the hysterectomy highway.

Once I listened to the advise of my fellow journeywomen, each day brought not only healing, but peace as well. Soon the pain gave way to the joys and wonders brought by the birth of each new day.

A new perspective, a better attitude, aided whatever ailed. My sourpuss attitude lifted and benefits were soon realized. Once the hormonal hellion disappeared, the sweet spouse resurfaced. The rewards followed as my recovery transformed into pampering.

I awoke one morning to the sound of dishes clanking in the kitchen. Although only half awake, a smile washed over my face. The dishes were not being thrown in anger, but loaded with love. At the other end of the house, before he departed for another busy, full day at the office, my husband was unloading the dishwasher as well as reloading it with the sink full of dirty dishes. Whether me, my nagging, the surgery, or the recovery, something had whipped my husband into shape (however temporary it might be). As I lay there in bed, I recalled an earlier preoperative conversation.

"Honey don't get me any flowers while I am in the hospital and don't have them sent to the house afterwards."

He answered my command with his pat answer, "Okay, if you say so."

My husband has true integrity and is honest to a degree I never thought possible in a mere mortal. It was inspiring—and oh-so agitating. In the grocery store when I pull an item from the shelf and several aisles later decide against buying it, I put it, not where it originated but where my change of mind occurs. I am a grocery store stocker's worst nightmare. Inevitably my husband picks up the item and carries it across the store to its proper place. How noble can one get? I always justify my actions (or inaction) before his ensuing lecture begins.

"Darling, it's not that I am lazy or uncaring. I am

helping the economy by making certain the stockers have plenty of work and do not lose their jobs!"

Most of the time, I admire and respect his integrity except when flowers or gifts are the issue. In the past he had never kept his word—where this type of promise was involved. He knows the drill; each year our wedding anniversary freshens his memory, in case it ever fails.

"Honey, I know you always send a dozen roses on our anniversary, but please don't waste the money this year. They just die and then I get sad when it is time to throw them away," the conversation never changed.

"Okay, if you are sure you won't be upset or disappointed, I won't," he counters.

But every year without fail, no matter where we are, no matter what we are doing, the roses come. Though few things are certain in life, in my life there are two such things: A dozen roses on our anniversary and another dozen delivered on Valentine's Day.

This time was a different story altogether. I was flowerless and my husband was flawed! He had chosen my first major surgery to stay true blue to his word. Didn't he know better? Hadn't he been trained properly? Hadn't he learned the secret language of ladies? Didn't he learn along the way that there are times the word *don't* actually means *do*.

This is a perfect example of the silent language of sisterhood. Men should take heed. Often what some women say and what they actually desire (and expect) are entirely two different things. For instance, there are times when a woman says don't call; but if Ma Bell doesn't deliver a ring-a-ling the ding-a-ling suffers the consequences.

Upon hearing the phrase I don't want a birthday present, the husband better hustle about and get a gift bigger and better than the previous year. Dinner reservations better be made as soon as the words I am tired but I will cook this evening are uttered. The only time this woman doesn't mean the opposite of what she says is when magical phrases such as: *No! Not tonight! I'm not in the mood!* or *I have a headache!* are flatly stated and reiterated. As my husband can verify testing the significance of these phrases cause pain.

Bearing the Big H

So the fact that our coffee table was void of petals, blossoms, blooms and/or long stems caused bitter feelings the first week of my recuperation. A period of thunderous silence ensued as my husband paid the ultimate price for failing his course study of Irrational Ravings 101. I was disappointed and he was confused. He had done (out of fear of my recuperation wrath) what I had asked him to do. In his male mind, he was just trying again to please me and grant my wish. Will they ever learn? Could not the cavemen read the writing on the walls? Did they not pass down their life lessons?

Having been married the majority of his adult life, I was certain my husband had come to understand women, their secret language, its hidden meanings (Yeah right). But I was wrong. I don't think men are genetically geared for unlocking this code.

Yet I wasn't disappointed my spouse had done exactly, as asked and not brought me flowers for one very good reason—denial. I held on to hope until the bitter end. Oh there was a little grief as I was wheeled through the hospital corridors with empty arms as other patients cooed over their carnations and bubbled over bouquets from devoted spouses. Once loaded into the car for the trip home from the hospital, my focus shifted from pity to the positive: no flowers meant no worries over wilting posies along the way. Honestly though I remained optimistic. A long recovery meant a large window of opportunity. There was plenty of time for my husband to come through.

On the way home from the hospital it hit me. Yes, I was sure he would try to surprise me. Come to think of it, this was just his style, let me be disappointed and then fill me with flowers. Before I arrived at our destination, I envisioned the scene waiting at our home. A sparkling clean house, complete with crisp fresh sheets on our bed. Oh yes, the flowers. There will be a big, beautiful, breathtaking bouquet just waiting to greet me as I waddled in the door. Beautiful, long-stemmed red roses in the bedroom and a spring bouquet on the coffee table to cheer me up while recuperating in the living room. So many flowers! The aroma so strong the honeybees would be buzzing at our doors. The anticipation and excitement mounted with every mile.

Once I opened the front door and entered our humble abode, I discovered the truth—Wrong! How wrong I was. Not only was the house petal poor but get-well cards were absent as well. Gifts, perfectly wrapped in soft pastel paper, did not decorate the nightstand. The house was dirtier than I had remembered. After leaving the sterile hospital environment, I was now expected to lay my battered body on dirty bed-sheets and walk across a dirty floor decked with dog hair and feline fur.

However my saner and softer side saw things entirely different, realizing the greatest gift my husband could give me he had. It was not in the form of flowers that would soon wither, die and be discarded. Rather, it was found in his undying love and devotion. It was his presence and patience throughout the years leading up to the operation. It was his compassion during the flashfloods caused by the overflowing river of PMS-induced tears; his concern during the pain-filled periods; his tolerance during the weekly hormonal uprisings, and my emotional mania. The fact is he was there—always beside me, always with me-through it all. And although he may not be able to fully comprehend womanhood and all its idiosyncrasies, still he stays; still his love prevails where understanding may fail.

The night of my surgery I slept, although not a sound sleep. I would wake to medicate myself, but only after I searched through the darkness for the image of my husband huddled nearby. Then, only when I found his sleeping body twisted in a nearby tiny recliner, would I medicate myself and doze back off.

I don't know if I woke so often that night out of con-cern for his comfort or just for reassurance of his presence. It was probably a combination of both. Two nights he stayed. Not only the nights, but all through the days he stayed, as if I was all that mattered, the center of his universe, as if the rest of his world did not exist. From four o'clock in the morn-ing Thursday until I left at noon the following Saturday, he left my side only for food and a change of clothing. It was evident that I had been given a get-well gift, the most loving and lasting kind.

Hint 2: It's not the destination, but the journey that matters most.

Life goes on even after a trip on the hysterectomy highway. In my case, I can fortunately say a much nicer life. In my humble opinion, there should be a song about life after a hysterectomy. I could hear it now; the lyrics set to a snazzy and snappy tune: No more tampons, no more pads, maxis, or the minis. I am much finer for gone are the liners. Past are the mishaps, Midol and misery. Oh, but what a wombless wonder am I.

Hint 3: The rearview mirror reflects that which is passed and past.

As crazy as it may sound, there is one thing I do miss about the curse. Without menstruation comes added responsibility. The end of the monthly Mother Nature visits means the end of all those lovely feminine excuses I have been using for everything from weight gain to sexual dysfunction, mental instability, and emotional imbalance. This all leads to the discovery of a correlation between age and creativity. It's amazing, as my body developed and changed from childhood to puberty through menopause so did my coping skills. Tracking my own "tools of the trade" I find my excuses change throughout life, each life-altering circumstance presenting its own unique justification. Through the years mine range from the extraordinaire to the extreme; from the devil made me do it, to the period plausible, to menopausal mania.

I miss the exclusivity of the feminine excuse. To me, it was the biggest bonus and the best part of being a woman. It almost countered the painful parts. But no more using my time of the month as an excuse for such things as craving and cramming chocolate down at record-breaking speed or delaying the wifely duties. The extent of this loss was realized shortly after surgery.

I was grouchy and irritable, making my husband miserable. Not yet adjusted to my new status and out of sheer habit I made a comment, which had become my natural defense the majority of the year.

"Leave me alone. It's my time of the month!" I snapped at my husband when he inquired as to my attitude.

Upon hearing those words, a smile immediately came upon his face. He had waited a very long time to say the words that followed. Smiling like a Chestier cat, he simply said, "WRONG! That one won't work any longer."

Early in recovery (before my husband became the wiser) another excuse for my irrational behavior presented itself.

"My hormones are out of whack." This one worked wonders for a while, until my spouse got fed up and pushed me into hormone replacement therapy. He had too much time, money and effort invested in straightening out the ups and downs, leveling out my mood swings and eliminating *the* excuse. But months later another excuse surfaced, a different sort, a more creative, more imaginative one.

"Honey, I think I am having phantom cramps," justifying my sorry golf game and the ensuing poor sportsmanship.

He didn't buy that one either, refusing to budge one bit. Once and for all, he set the record straight on my womanly excuses.

"That PMS ploy will no longer work, and since you're taking hormones neither will your usual excuse of *It's my hormones, Honey.* It is my honor and a real pleasure to inform you that no longer do you have any excuses, at least of the feminine type."

How insensitive of him! It seemed as if he got real pleasure from presenting that information to me. I couldn't believe it! That brute! That bully!

With the removal of my worrisome womb came renewed hope that with time, my intimate side would return (if ever it had existed). It was a long time before the full benefits of surgery became apparent, but none was more welcomed than in the bedroom. As the days turned to weeks and the weeks turned to months and summer gave way to fall, unfamiliarity invaded our lovemaking. Surgery eliminated more than the obvious. It removed the tension, apprehension, and fear of the physical pain associated with sex. This has a profound trickle effect.

Without the cloud of worry, physical pain and pressures from intercourse hanging overhead, sex has trans-

formed into lovemaking. My entire sexual appetite and attitude have changed. No longer is sex viewed as a marital
must. It is an intimate and vital part of marriage, a physical
expression of the sharing, caring, and loving.

Hint 4: Overcoming one obstacle doesn't guarantee a
hazard-free highway.

Unfortunately, losing a womb does not mean losing all
feminine foes. While traveling the hormonal highway, I stumbled onto some interesting information. Hormone therapy is
a real peculiar animal, a sort of a switch-hitter available in
various forms, taken at one end and applied in the other.

Less than one year after surgery, symptoms of what I
thought were the yeasty-beasty invaded my private parts. I
plunged right in and bought the tried-and-true eradication
method of vaginal cream. After the oozing ordeal, not much
relief was noticed. The burning was still bothersome.

So I called my gyno. And dear doc gave me a prescription for the newest in yeast control, the one dosage pill,
oral pill that is. Again I rushed out and plopped down the
dough for the pricey little pill. But again, the irritation kept
on irritating. After investing in two, count them, two appli-
cations of anti-yeast concoctions, he sent out yet another prescription. This all was beginning to add up and my patience
with the problem was wearing thin.

Once again I went to the pharmacy and picked up my
prescription. Eager for relief, I tore into the box of cream as
soon as I walked in our home. It was then that I noticed
something very strange. The name of the cream was identical to the name of my hormone pills. Could it be that this
magical medicine, which worked wonders on mood and temperature control, could be a promising potion, producing
harmony in any form and fashion? First a pill, now a cream.
One to be taken orally and the other to be plunged vaginal-
ly. It was becoming evident that this hormonal highway
stretched the entire length of the body, encompassing orifices
at both ends.

Within days, the dose did its duty and I was back to
normal. After discussing the situation with my gynecologist,
I discovered the true culprit. It seems that my yeast infection

was not a fungus fiasco after all, but an irritation caused by vaginal dryness. This was one of the hysterectomy side effects I did encounter. Little did I know that vaginal dryness could lead to more feminine problems.

I didn't know what it was because I didn't know it was happening. I just chalked the "friction" up to my lack of sparks. With my wanton desires waning, foreplay consisted of getting undressed and me assuming my position. Of course, my lack of sexual desire (at this particular point) could also be attributed to a very convenient and well-documented side effect of the hysterectomy: lack of libido. And I thought all my female problems would be eliminated with my female organs. Silly girl!

Hint 5: Make the time to make the trip.

Did I mention that recovery is a slow process? Yeah, I know about a hundred times. (So to make sure it sticks in the mind, make this the 101st. time). There are some effects of surgery that are far-reaching and time defying. The incision was either tender, numb or both for an entire year. When it was numb, it felt icky to touch the area. It was a strange feeling, rubbing the skin and not feeling it. I didn't like not feeling my touch. It was a weird sensation. And speaking of touch, there wasn't munchin' of any touchin' the first year following surgery. It took a full year for my husband to broach that invisible barrier, the two-foot safety zone erected around my abdomen. Breaching the confines of this zone, an alarm would sound and my spouse would be hit with a stiff arm. It was an automatic reaction. The incision area was tender to the touch for a long, long time. I wanted nothing and no one around my waist, for a long period. Of course this is a good excuse to take a vacation from the restricting, confining and bothersome elastic-banded panties and pantyhose.

Hint 6: It's easier, safer and wiser to go around a wall than trying to plow through it.

It's important to determine friends and foes of the feminine woes. And where a hysterectomy is concerned there ain't no doubt the vacuum cleaner is most assuredly a foe. I learned the hard way sucking dirt duty was off-limits for a good, long while, some wise women claim forever. As soon as my six-week sabbatical was over, I was up and at 'em making up for lost time. This domestic goddess was set on doing her duty. The carpet was growing fungus resembling shag carpet. It was time to vacuum now that I was able to resume *all* activities. I had invested in a new vacuum cleaner earlier that year. Intent on pitching pennies, I insisted we buy a model, which had all the bells and whistles but was not self-propelled.

Shortly after mowing the carpet, I encountered a setback. I began experiencing constant pain. It was then that my former boss' wife enlightened me with a small bit of advice my male doctor failed to provide. This was something only a female physician would think to pass along to a patient.

"You aren't vacuuming, are you?"

"Yes, I am. The doctor said I could resume normal activities after six weeks, and it's time. And vacuuming is normal activity to me."

"Oh, no. That is the worst thing you could do to your recovery," she explained. "My doctor instructed me not to vacuum for the first three months."

"By any chance, is your gynecologist a woman?" I was right, it was woman-to-woman advice.

Hint 7: It's the treasures from the trip that make the journey worth traveling.

I actually matured from this event. I'm not just wombless, but wiser as well. This anatomical alteration taught me even more lessons and reiterated others. For starters, it burst my equality bubble. There is no equality between the sexes, never has been never will be. Periods, pains, pregnancy, and PMS are all measurements of the width of the gender gap, the height of the *herdles*.

The aging process is yet another example of what I call gender injustice. Age affects women in every form, showing in every fashion. With the passage of time skin creases, boobs sag, upper arms flap, butts drag, chins, double then triple, eyelids droop and tummies pooch, all with the threat of menopause looming overhead.

Time causes many men only a teeny-weeny problem; and a course a drug has conveniently been created to correct their dilemma. One dose of Viagra and voila, it is up and at it again!

Women, on the other hand, have no age-defying *miracle* cures. We must resort to the more drastic and painful cosmetic surgery routine. With a tug here and tuck there, a stretch up there and a lift in between, a few thousand dollars and several months later and we are set to sag all over again! But no one ever said life was fair.

I think that men really are from a different planet and were beamed down here to challenge women and their rational, emotionally based thought process. The frustration takes its toll on many women as I have sadly witnessed first-hand. It drives some nuts, and it drives others in search for answers. My dear friend, so desperate she is set on going straight to the top in her quest for an answer.

"You know, when I get to Heaven and see God, the first thing I am going to ask Him is why in the world He made men so different from women!"

That is providing, of course, she doesn't kill her husband and end up going in the opposite direction.

I believe girlfriends are gifts meant to keep me sane. My friends have become my mile-markers along the highway of life, lighthouses illuminating my way, keeping me on course when the stormy gale-force winds of life knock me down, push me off my path. They are necessary to my survival; their unique understanding provides me with comfort. My girlfriends are an accurate assessment of my emotional and mental well-being. They can always relate.

Those times when my husband has no clue as to what I am saying and looks at me as if I am a speaking a foreign language, I reach out to someone that speaks my language, can relate, knows exactly where I am coming from and exactly what I mean. Depending on who is home, the girlfriend may change, but the topic and tone are usually the same:

"Hey there, girlfriend. I know you are busy but I have to dispense with some steam! Why is it that men think intercourse and intimacy are synonyms, used exclusively as verbs are only *action* words. And will he ever learn that boobs are breast for nursing not handles for holding! Okay so you now know how my night went last night! Does the problem lie with men or women?"

In those rare unfortunate cases where I am feeling insane and a friend can't be found, womanly wisdom lets me know I am okay. Over the years I have learned that for the most part, those things that I can't understand can usually be chalked up to being just a man's thang.

Hint 8: The hardest part of life is learning to live.

Those rumors about the menopause mayhem in my case are unfounded. My life is nicer now. I have become very accustomed to the change. So much so that my one-year anniversary of my surgery almost slipped by without fanfare. I wanted to celebrate the occasion with cake, candles, champagne, and the whole nine yards. However, the timing was off because on the occasion we were visiting my brother-in-law at his home. It was my first visit, and as such it may have been a little too much for him.

So I celebrated quietly, only mentioning the monumental occasion in passing to my husband who obviously lacked the enthusiasm such an event should have generated. I couldn't blame him, though. I barely noticed the fact three hundred sixty-five days of my life passed without a womb. I was living quite well, thank you very much. There were only slight, subtle differences in life now. The family calendar is no longer littered with markings of a red "p" signaling Mother Nature's arrival and warning my husband to take cover and stay clear or suffer the wrath of the impending PMS, mood swings, and aches and pains.

Long-term, there are some minor side effects of having a hysterectomy. My physical endurance, energy level, and stamina have all declined recently. Of course, this too could be contributed to the advancement of the golden years and the approaching "over-the-hill" birthday.

Mental and emotional changes have taken place, as well. I feel better and think I look better (that may be only my opinion, but it is the only one which matters in this instance). I have begun to enjoy life instead of being plagued by it, living instead of existing. It came to me so eloquently one day during a walk in the wilderness: Life is not a burden to be carried, but a gift to be treasured.

I look forward to aging gracefully which is 180 degrees opposite of my attitude a year ago as I first set out on this life-altering journey. Then I viewed surgical menopause as the first in the long, lengthy, and scary aging process. I was frightened by the future, scared that unlike fine wine and cheese, I would not get better with age but meld into a moldy mess. However, through this surgery my sights softened.

This operation presented me something I am very thankful for: down time. Before the operation I had become overwhelmed, consumed by life and all its responsibilities. Within a three-month period I had started a new job, gotten married, moved into a new home, all this without stopping.

Recovery gave me the chance to catch my breath, to see my life in another light. It forced me to step back and take a survey—to realign, reinforce and renew my priorities, my purpose, and my life. For me surgery was the perfect excuse to let go and learn to say no to all those unimportant time-consuming commitments and undeserving obligations. It allotted me the means and the manner to fade into the background, to say farewell to my professional life and focus on my personal life. I was free to follow my dreams, catch a cloud, stretch for the stars. This was not an end, but a new beginning for me and mine. And I embrace the time, and the limitless possibilities with the eagerness of a child, with the will of a woman.

For copies of this book and other Big H products
visit our website at www.thebigh.com
Copies may also be ordered by sending $19.95
(includes shipping and handling) to:
Destiny Publications
P.O. Box 270242
Flower Mound, Texas 75027-0242
or by calling 1-800-256-5173